OUR LIVING CONSTITUTION
THEN AND NOW

by
Jerry Aten

illustrated by Kathryn Hyndman

Cover by Kathryn Hyndman

Copyright © Good Apple, Inc., 1987

GOOD APPLE, INC.
BOX 299
CARTHAGE, IL 62321-0299

Copyright © Good Apple, Inc., 1987

ISBN No. 0-86653-386-9

Printing No. 98765432

GOOD APPLE, INC.
BOX 299
CARTHAGE, IL 62321-0299

TABLE OF CONTENTS

111483

INTRODUCTION

The Constitution of the United States is perhaps *the* single most imitated political document in the world. It has survived as our blueprint of government for 200 years. No other document anywhere can claim such enduring credentials. It is so important that most school systems include it as a part of the curriculum. But teaching the Constitution as it was written is no easy matter. It is a complex document written in legalistic language that makes it difficult for children to understand. The whole purpose of this book is to make passing on its rich and timeless message a little easier and more meaningful to the next generation.

The design of the lessons begins with a word of introduction and explanation. This is followed by a two-column layout. The paragraph, clause or section of the Constitution as it was written appears in the left column; an explanation in language students will understand is found in the column on the right. At the end of each lesson are discussion and thought-provoking questions that relate to the material just presented. The research projects and other activities will add even more enrichment to the experience of the material just presented. The lessons vary in length—some taking less than a class period to cover, while others require as much as three class periods plus outside work.

To put things into proper historical perspective, the book begins with a study of the Declaration of Independence. When students become aware of the difficulty the colonies had in gaining their freedom, they will have a greater appreciation of the Constitution. They will see how Shays' Rebellion clearly showed dissatisfaction among the people and how the Articles of Confederation just did not work as a framework of government. They will see how change became necessary and how the Constitution evolved through the cooperation and compromise of some highly intelligent and very determined statesmen. Finally, they will draw conclusions on why and how this precious document of ours has survived for 200 years with only a few changes. One of the main focuses of the book is to show them how the Constitution relates to our lives today and how it serves us in the society in which we live.

When the entire study of the Constitution has been completed, the exciting game We the People can be used to provide a comprehensive review for a final examination. There are forty game cards, each containing four questions. The correct answers are on the backs of the cards. The format allows for the game's use by the entire class or as a competition between students working in pairs. A complete answer key containing suggested responses to all the questions is also included.

The Constitution as a separate unit can be studied any time during the year, but perhaps it becomes most meaningful to students when presented in its proper chronological segments of time in the story of America.

With proper background on how it evolved, they will better see the cause for many of the passages contained in the Constitution. Studying the Constitution at this point will also help them to gain a more meaningful grasp of the changes that have occurred since. Using the book as a resource will help your students to better appreciate their American heritage. Proper study of its blueprint for government is a part of good citizenship and should not be passed over lightly.

Although the Declaration of Independence and the U.S. Constitution were written for different purposes and under different conditions, the two documents have certain common grounds and ties together. The Declaration is for the most part a list of the reasons the colonists decided to break away from England. The fact that this declaration was made, however, did not make the colonists necessarily free. They knew they would have to earn their independence through the long and bitter struggle of the Revolutionary War.

Once the fight was won, it was time to set forth the principles that would run the new government. The intent was to lay down some rules that would give them enough control to prevent the government from infringing on their lives as King George had done. Their plan—the Articles of Confederation—did not work. It placed so many restrictions on the central government that there was no strength in its framework. That document was eventually replaced by the Constitution, a masterpiece of government that has survived 200 years and still stands strong. As you prepare to study the Constitution, it is helpful to take a look first at the Declaration of Independence. You will see how the men who wrote the Constitution during that hot summer of 1787 were influenced by the words of the Declaration. You will also see how the complaints registered in the Declaration were answered and presented for future generations as they were dealt with in the Constitution.

With Lexington and its aftermath still ringing in their ears, the delegates of the Continental Congress began taking bold strides toward independence even though many still felt there could be ways to patch up their differences with England. Finally, on June 7, 1776, Richard Henry Lee of Virginia rose before the delegates and proposed his famous motion "That these United Colonies are, and of right ought to be, free and independent States. . . ." His motion was seconded by John Adams of Massachusetts, but final voting did not occur until July 2, when the Congress voted in favor of independence.

A committee was appointed to write a declaration of independence explaining to the world the reasons for the colonies taking such a drastic step. That committee was composed of John Adams, Benjamin Franklin, Robert Livingston, Roger Sherman, and Thomas Jefferson. The committee turned to Jefferson to refine their ideas into a final document. No better choice could have been made. At the age of thirty-three, Jefferson was already recognized for his brilliance as an inventor and statesman. Although he wasn't a very good public speaker, he wrote extremely well. When he had finished, he had no idea that what he had written would be regarded historically as one of the most beautifully written documents of all time.

His work was adopted on July 4, 1776, by Congress. A white-wigged gentleman solemnly read the words to an anxious Philadelphia crowd. When he was finished, the people cheered and bells rang out all over the city. The colonists were aware of the grim task that lay before them. But they were convinced that the risks were worth the chance to be free from the harsh rule of the British crown.

As you read the following pages, you will find the original words of Thomas Jefferson in the left-hand column. After reading a paragraph from this side, read the paragraph in the right-hand column to get a more easily understood explanation. Also become aware as you read the five separate parts of the Declaration, that each serves a specific purpose. As you analyze the timeless passages of this document, make note of the specific purpose served by each of these parts: Preamble, statement of basic human rights, charges against the king and Parliament, statement of separation, signatures. Headings have been provided to show you the separation between the parts.

Benjamin Franklin

Thomas Jefferson

John Adams

Roger Sherman

Robert Livingston

DECLARATION OF INDEPENDENCE

In Congress, July 4, 1776. The unanimous declaration of the thirteen United States of America,

When in the Course of human events, it becomes necessary for one people to dissolve the political bands which have connected them with another, and to assume among the powers of the earth, the separate and equal station to which the Laws of Nature and of Nature's God entitle them, a decent respect to the opinions of mankind requires that they should declare the causes which impel them to the separation.

Preamble

All thirteen states of America were in agreement to making this declaration on July 4, 1776.

Whenever it becomes necessary for one nation or group of people to declare itself free from the rule of another, then a common decency to the opinions of all other people requires that an explanation of the reasons for the declaration be made.

We hold these truths to be self-evident, that all men are created equal, that they are endowed by their Creator with certain unalienable Rights, that among these are Life, Liberty, and the pursuit of Happiness.

Statement of Human Rights

We believe these truths to be so obvious that they need no proof: That all people are created equal; that God gives all of us certain rights that cannot be taken away; that among these rights are life, liberty, and the freedom to find happiness.

That to secure these rights, Governments are instituted among Men, deriving their just powers from the consent of the governed.

To make certain these rights are protected and preserved for the people, governments are created. Those governments get this source of power from the people.

That whenever any Form of Government becomes destructive of these ends, it is the Right of the People to alter or to abolish it, and to institute new Government, laying its foundation on such principles and organizing its powers in such form, as to them shall seem most likely to effect their Safety and Happiness. Prudence, indeed, will dictate that Governments long established should not be changed for light and transient causes; and accordingly all experience hath shewn, that mankind are more disposed to suffer, while evils are sufferable, than to right themselves by abolishing the forms to which they are accustomed. But when a long train of abuses and usurpations, pursuing invariably the same Object evinces a design to reduce them under absolute Despotism, it is their right, it is their duty, to throw off such government, and to provide new Guards for their future security.

Such has been the patient sufferance of these Colonies; and such is now the necessity which constrains them to alter their former Systems of Government. The history of the present King of Great Britain is a history of repeated injuries and usurpations, all having in direct object the establishment of an absolute Tyranny over these States. To prove this, let Facts be submitted to a candid world.

If a government abuses this power, then the people have a right to change their government or get rid of it completely and start a new government that will better suit their needs. Common sense would tell us that an established government should not be overthrown for minor reasons. It is the nature of man to tolerate mistreatment rather than get rid of something he is used to and start a new government. But sometimes a government will go too far in abusing the rights of the people.

When this happens, it is not only the people's right, but their duty to overthrow the current government and set up a new government that will better protect their precious personal rights.

Such has been the case thus far with the thirteen colonies. They have suffered patiently. But they now are convinced that they must change their government and must no longer accept the rule of King George III of England. He has a history of bad rule that abused the rights of the colonists and placed them completely under his control. To prove this, let the facts of his record present themselves to an unbiased world.

Charges Against King George and Parliament

He has refused his Assent to Laws, the most wholesome and necessary for the public good.

He has refused to pass laws necessary for the good of the people.

He has forbidden his Governors to pass Laws of immediate and pressing importance, unless suspended in their operation till his Assent should be obtained; and when so suspended, he has utterly neglected to attend to them.

He has prevented those assigned to act as governors of the colonies from enforcing laws until he has approved them; and then he has neglected his duty to approve those laws.

He has refused to pass other Laws for the accommodation of large districts of people, unless those people would relinquish the right of Representation in the Legislature, a right inestimable to them and formidable to tyrants only.

He has refused to approve of laws needed to govern large groups of people unless these people are willing to give up their right to be represented in the legislature. This right is valuable to them and presents a threat to no one but a tyrant like himself.

He has called together legislative bodies at places unusual, uncomfortable, and distant from the depository of their public Records, for the sole purpose of fatiguing them into compliance with his measures.

He has called meetings of the legislature together in unusual places that are inconvenient to get to and often far distant from access to public records. His purpose in doing so has been to tire the legislators and make them more agreeable to the laws he wants passed.

He has dissolved Representative Houses repeatedly, for opposing with manly firmness his invasions on the rights of the people.

He has suspended those colonial legislatures that have dared to defy his rule by opposing laws he wanted passed—laws that were obvious invasions on the rights of people.

He has refused for a long time, after such dissolutions, to cause others to be elected; whereby the Legislative powers, incapable of Annihilation, have returned to the People at large for their exercise; the State remaining in the mean time exposed to all the dangers of invasion from without, and convulsions within.

Once those legislatures were dissolved, he refused to allow new legislators to be elected. As a result of this, the power to make laws, which cannot be destroyed, has returned to the people. That society without proper leadership is vulnerable to attack by outsiders and leaves a state of lawlessness and rebellion within.

He has endeavoured to prevent the population of these States; for that purpose obstructing the Laws for Naturalization of Foreigners; refusing to pass others to encourage their migrations hither, and raising the conditions of new Appropriations of Lands.

He has tried to prevent expansion from within the colonies in a number of ways: he has made difficult the naturalization of foreigners; he has refused to pass laws that would make immigration here more appealing; he has changed the conditions for acquiring new lands.

He has obstructed the Administration of Justice, by refusing his Assent to Laws for establishing Judiciary powers.

He has made it increasingly difficult for justice to prevail by refusing to approve of laws that would give power to the courts.

He has made Judges dependent on his Will alone, for the tenure of their offices, and the amount and payment of their salaries.

He has placed political pressure on judges by making their jobs and salaries solely dependent on their interpreting the laws through his wishes.

He has erected a multitude of New Offices, and sent hither swarms of Officers to harass our people, and eat out their substance.

He has created many new positions in government, then filled them with his own people who are sent among the colonists to harass them. And through all this, the people are still expected to pay the higher taxes that will support the salaries of these government workers.

He has kept among us, in times of peace, Standing Armies without the Consent of our legislatures.

He has kept standing armies of soldiers among us during times of peace without the approval of the legislature.

He has affected to render the Military independent of and superior to the Civil power.

He has tried to make the military independent of and superior to the civilian power of the people.

He has combined with others to subject us to a jurisdiction foreign to our constitution, and unacknowledged by our laws; giving his Assent to their Acts of pretended Legislation:

For quartering large bodies of armed troops among us:

For protecting them, by a mock Trial, from punishment for any Murders which they should commit on the Inhabitants of these States:

For cutting off our Trade with all parts of the world:

For imposing Taxes on us without our Consent:

For depriving us in many cases, of the benefits of Trial by Jury:

For transporting us beyond Seas to be tried for pretended offenses:

He has also committed several injustices to the people while working with Parliament. The result is a government in which the people have no voice. He has approved of those laws made by Parliament, but those laws are of no value to the colonists because they were made without the people having any voice in their creation. Here are some of the injustices done by Parliament and King George III.

They have kept armed soldiers quartered in our homes.

They have protected those soldiers from punishment through a mock trial even when they committed murders against the inhabitants. (The specific reference to this charge is the phoney trial that resulted from the Boston Massacre.)

They have stopped us from trading with many other countries by forcing us to trade only with England.

They have levied taxes against us without our consent.

They have on many occasions deprived us of the right to trial by jury.

They have transported some of our people all the way back to England to face charges that were trumped up to find ways to deal with those who have caused them trouble.

For abolishing the free System of English Laws in a neighbouring Province, establishing therein an Arbitrary government, and enlarging its Boundaries so as to render it at once an example and fit instrument for introducing the same absolute rule into these Colonies:

They abolished the free system of English Law in the Canadian province of Quebec, giving them instead a system of bad laws at the same time they enlarged that province. They have made it appear that they intend to impose the same type of bad rule in these colonies.

For taking away our Charters, abolishing our most valuable Laws, and altering fundamentally the Forms of our Governments:

They have taken away our charters abolishing our most precious and important laws. Without such laws, the governments are changed considerably.

For suspending our own Legislatures, and declaring themselves invested with power to legislate for us in all cases whatsoever.

They have kept our legislatures from meeting, declaring themselves as the lawmaking body with the power to make our laws for us.

He has abdicated Government here by declaring us out of his Protection and waging War against us.

The King has given up his power to govern us, because he has refused to protect us and has waged war against us.

He has plundered our seas, ravaged our Coasts, burnt our towns, and destroyed the lives of our people.

He has attacked our ships and coastlines and has burned our towns and "destroyed" the ability of the people to make lives for themselves.

He is at this time transporting large Armies of foreign Mercenaries to compleat the works of death, desolation and tyranny, already begun with circumstances of Cruelty & perfidy scarcely paralleled in the most barbarous ages, and totally unworthy the Head of a civilized nation.

He has hired large armies of mercenary soldiers to come here to fight against us and continue his works of treachery. His cruel and barbaric acts make him totally unworthy of his title and unfit to rule a civilized nation.

He has constrained our fellow Citizens taken Captive on the high Seas to bear Arms against their Country, to become the executioners of their friends and Brethren, or to fall themselves by their Hands.

He has forced our fellow Americans whom he has captured on the high seas to fight against other Americans.

He has excited domestic insurrections amongst us, and has endeavoured to bring on the inhabitants of our frontiers, the merciless Indian Savages, whose known rule of warfare, is an undistinguished destruction of all ages, sexes and conditions.

In every stage of these Oppressions We have Petitioned for Redress in the most humble terms: Our repeated Petitions have been answered only by repeated injury. A Prince, whose character is thus marked by every act which may define a Tyrant, is unfit to be the ruler of a free people.

Nor have We been wanting in attentions to our British brethren. We have warned them from time to time of attempts by their legislature to extend an unwarrantable jurisdiction over us.

We have reminded them of the circumstances of our emigration and settlement here.

We have appealed to their native justice and magnanimity, and we have conjured them by the ties of our common kindred to disavow these usurpations, which would inevitably interrupt our connections and correspondence. They too have been deaf to the voice of justice and of consanguinity.

We must, therefore, acquiesce in the necessity, which denounces our Separation, and hold them, as we hold the rest of mankind, Enemies in War, in Peace Friends.

He has incited some of the colonists to rebel against their own colonial governments. He has aroused the Indians to our borders to complete savage attacks against our people.

During the entire period of these injustices, we begged him to listen in the most humble of terms. Every plea was only met with another injury. From this action it is quite obvious that this king is a tyrant and unfit to rule a free people.

We have appealed to our British brethren. We have warned them from time to time about how we feel about the rule of Parliament and the King.

We have reminded them that we are still their kin who came here in search of a new chance and better life.

We have appealed to their common sense and compassion to do what is naturally right. We have called on their sense of common ties with us, telling them that a continuation of these actions would result in our breaking our common bond with them. Our words have fallen on deaf ears.

We must therefore announce our separation from them and regard as we do the rest of mankind—enemies in war, friends in peace.

9

We, therefore, the Representatives of the United States of America, in General Congress, Assembled, appealing to the Supreme Judge of the world for the rectitude of our intentions, do, in the Name, and by Authority of the good People of these Colonies, solemnly publish and declare, That these United Colonies are, and of Right ought to be Free and Independent States; that they are Absolved from all Allegiance to the British Crown, and that all political connection between them and the State of Great Britain, is and ought to be totally dissolved;

and that as Free and Independent States, they have full Power to levy War, conclude Peace, contract Alliances, establish Commerce, and to do all other Acts and Things which Independent States may of right do.

And for the support of this Declaration, with a firm reliance on the protection of divine Providence, we mutually pledge to each other our Lives, our Fortunes and our sacred Honor.

Statement of Separation

Therefore as the representatives of the people meeting in this Congress, we appeal to God for approval of our actions. We thus solemnly declare that these united colonies are and of right ought to be free and independent states,

that they no longer owe any loyalty to the English King and that all political ties with Great Britain are totally dissolved.

That as free and independent states they have the power to wage war, make peace, make alliances with other nations, promote trade and do all the other things that free and independent states have the right to do.

And in full support of this Declaration, with a firm reliance on the protection of God, we mutually pledge to each other our lives, our destinies and our sacred honor.

SIGNATURES

REMEMBERING KEY PHRASES

Tell in which part of the Declaration each of the following is located by matching the correct letter. If you are familiar with the purpose of each part of the Declaration, you won't even need to use your notes.

a. charges against King George   b. statement of basic human rights
c. Preamble   d. statement of separation

e. signer of the Declaration

1. _____ We hold these truths to be self-evident . . . .

2. _____ . . . we mutually pledge to each other our Lives . . . .

3. _____ He has plundered our seas, ravaged our Coasts . . . .

4. _____ He has dissolved Representative Houses . . . .

5. _____ . . . they should declare the causes which impel them to the separation.

6. _____ Prudence, indeed, will dictate that governments long established governments should not be changed for light and transient causes . . . .

7. _____ . . . that these United Colonies are, and of Right ought to be, Free . . . .

8. _____ He has kept among us, in times of peace, Standing Armies . . . .

9. _____ John Hancock

10. _____ . . . for imposing Taxes upon us without our Consent.

11. _____ A Prince, whose character is marked by every act which may define a Tyrant, is unfit to be the ruler of a free people.

12. _____ . . . to secure the rights, Governments are instituted among Men . . . .

13. _____ When in the Course of human events . . . .

14. _____ Charles Carroll of Carrollton

15. _____ He has excited domestic insurrections amongst us . . . .

WE HOLD THESE TRUTHS . . .

Choose from the list of words that are found in the Declaration the appropriate letters of the words that match the phrases in italic print.

a. perfidy
b. harass
c. convulsions
d. annihilation
e. mercenaries

f. endowed
g. transient
h. acquiesce
i. consanguinity
j. prudence

k. endeavoured
l. evinces
m. unwarrantable
n. redress
o. magnanimity

1. _____ He has hired armies of *paid soldiers.*

2. _____ . . . the State remaining exposed to all dangers of invasion from without, and *violent disturbances* within.

3. _____ In every stage of these Oppressions We have Petitioned for *correction of these wrongs* in the most humble terms . . . .

4. _____ *Common sense* indeed, will tell us that Governments long established will not be changed for light and transient causes . . . .

5. _____ They too have been deaf to the voice of justice and of *blood relationship.*

6. _____ We have warned them from time to time of attempts . . . to extend an *unjustifiable* jurisdiction over us.

7. _____ He has erected a multitude of New Offices, and sent hither swarms of Officers to *persecute* our people . . . .

8. _____ He has excited domestic insurrections amongst us, and has *tried* to bring on the inhabitants of our frontier . . . .

9. _____ . . . that all men are created equal, that they are *blessed with* by their Creator with certain unalienable Rights . . . .

10. _____ . . . the Legislative powers, incapable of *being destroyed* . . . .

11. _____ We must, therefore, *agree* in the necessity which denounces our separation.

12. _____ We have appealed to their native justice and *courageous spirit* . . . .

13. _____ But when a long train of abuses . . . *clearly shows* a design to reduce them . . . .

14. _____ He is . . . transporting large Armies of foreign Mercenaries to compleat the works . . . of Cruelty and *treachery scarcely unparalleled* . . . .

15. _____ Prudence . . . will dictate that governments long established should not be changed for light and *trifling* causes . . . .

OUR BASIC HUMAN RIGHTS

1. According to Thomas Jefferson, what were the three basic human rights to which all of us are entitled by the mere fact that we exist?

   _____

   _____

   _____

2. How did it happen that Jefferson ended up drafting the entire Declaration by himself, when a committee of five had been assigned the job?

   _____

   _____

   _____

   _____

   _____

3. According to the words of Thomas Jefferson, when do the people of a nation have the right to change their government by abandoning a system they do not like?

   _____

   _____

   _____

4. From where do governments derive their power to make the laws that govern people?

   _____

   _____

5. Do you agree with Jefferson's statement that all men are created equal? Develop an explanatory paragraph of your thoughts with justification for your answer.

_____

_____

_____

_____

_____

_____

6. Benjamin Franklin remarked at the signing of the Declaration that ". . . we must indeed all hang together, or assuredly, we shall all hang separately." What did Franklin mean by this statement?_____

_____

_____

_____

7. The name of John Hancock is the first to appear among the signers of the Declaration. His name has become so famous as a result that it is often used synonymously with the term *signature.* Research the circumstances surrounding Hancock's bold signature and tell how the word *signature* is associated with his name. _____

_____

_____

_____

★ THE ROAD TO CHANGE ★

During the Revolution the small farmer prospered. The British, the French, and the American armies all needed food and were willing to pay dearly for it. But when the war ended and the foreign armies went home, the demand for his crops dropped dramatically. In 1786 farmers in Massachusetts became enraged over low farm prices. The Revolution had been won, and with it came independence. But prosperity was far down the road for these poor farmers who owed huge amounts of money. They had no chance to pay off their debts because the state taxes they had to pay were high — yet the price they received for their crops was very low. Creditors began to seize their farms. They pleaded with the government for help, but none came.

Several of these men led by Daniel Shays took the matter into their own hands. They attempted to capture a U.S. arsenal but were beaten back by the Massachusetts Militia. Historically, the incident is known as Shays' Rebellion, but the implications of why it happened are far more important than the incident itself. As we examine the reasons for Americans fighting against each other, you will see why it became necessary to change the entire framework of the national government and that the attempt to change it is what led to the Constitution which has served us well for the last 200 years.

When the thirteen colonies had lived under English rule, they had functioned much as though they were thirteen separate little countries. Each had been established for economic or religious reasons all its own, and there was no real reason for them to unite in a common cause. The mistreatment they had experienced from King George was the cause that finally banded them together in their fight to be free. But once that fight was won and the war had ended, it was difficult for each to think of giving up its own special interests for the sake of a national government. The states pretty much went back to functioning as though they were thirteen separate nations. And that is where the problems began.

The Continental Congress had created the Articles of Confederation during the war to loosely tie the colonies together. Each state sent delegates, but the delegates had no real power. Every time an important vote came up, the delegates had to contact their individual states to find out how they should vote. No state was willing to give up its power for the sake of a strong central government. Finally, in 1781 the states agreed to a loose association that gave up only a few of their powers to the federal government, but they kept the most important powers for their own separate states. Such an arrangement is referred to as a *confederation,* and the document was called the *Articles of Confederation and Perpetual Union.*

The Confederation had no President nor were there any United States courts. The only branch of government was the Congress and it contained only one house. Each state voted as a single unit, but larger states did have more representatives than smaller states. Some of the powers the Congress had were to declare war, to receive foreign diplomats, to raise an army and navy, to control Indian affairs, to borrow money, to establish post offices, to fix standards of weights and measures.

But there were many other important powers which Congress did not have. Congress had no power to regulate trade among the states. Each state had its own trade laws and the tariff each imposed on others was often so high that trade was discouraged. Congress had no power to enforce the laws it did make. If the states didn't accept a law, they simply disobeyed it. Congress could not levy taxes. Therefore it could not pay the debts of the United States nor provide the goods and services a central government should provide for its people. Congress could not prevent the individual states from issuing their own money. This obviously presented a number of problems in exchange and value and further discouraged trade and travel among people in the various states. Congress had no power to defend any of the states separately or provide them with aid; nor could it act directly against individuals or states.

When comparing what Congress could do with what it could not do, it's quite obvious that the states were unwilling to give up any of their important powers to the central government under the Articles of Confederation. And that is the whole reason why that kind of government failed. The self-serving interests of the various states prevented them from acting other than as thirteen separate nations, and the United States was fast losing its credibility as a nation with the rest of the world.

With each passing year, the situation grew worse. Trade wars, boundary disputes and unrest among these people living in the United States caused many leaders to recognize a need for a stronger central government. George Washington took the initiative by inviting officials from Virginia and Maryland to his home at Mount Vernon to decide a way to settle a dispute between the two states over

George Washington

James Madison

Alexander Hamilton

William Paterson

Gouverneur Morris

George Wythe

the use of the Potomac River. The results brought about a second meeting at Annapolis, Maryland, in 1786, in which several other states sent representatives to talk about the trade and boundary problems generated by the philosophy of the Articles of Confederation. From that meeting came the call for a special convention to meet in Philadelphia in 1787 to revise the Articles of Confederation.

That convention gathered in May of 1787. There were representatives from all of the states except Rhode Island. Rhode Island refused to send any delegates because it feared the Convention would remove its power to tax the goods that passed through the state. The fifty-five who were there were indeed a distinguished body of political leaders. They were men of remarkable ability and had been carefully chosen by the states they represented.

The Convention promptly chose George Washington as president of the Convention. James Madison took copious notes for everything that was said and done at the Convention and became history's main source of information. There were also such distinguished men of the day as Benjamin Franklin, Alexander Hamilton, Roger Sherman, William Paterson and Gouverneur Morris (who actually put the document into its final form once all decisions had been made). As a group they were fairly young. Most of them were under the age of fifty. They were well-educated and represented several walks of life. There were lawyers and businessmen and southern plantation owners. Some had been members of the Confederation Congress. All of them had spent a part of their lives in service to the public. All of them represented backgrounds of at least moderate financial success.

Once the delegates began their discussions, they quickly realized that no amount of correcting the Articles of Confederation would give them the strong framework of central government the nation sorely needed. Thus, they decided to start all over and write an entirely new plan that would replace the Articles of Confederation. They also decided to work behind closed doors, preferring to wait until the entire Constitution was written—then to submit the entire document to the states and the people for their approval.

Their first major decision was to establish three branches of government: the legislative branch would make the laws and the executive branch would enforce them; the judicial branch would interpret the laws and try those accused of breaking them. They also agreed that a strong central government should be able to do almost all the things that the Articles of Confederation had not allowed. The delegates felt they should establish a *federal system* in which the power would be divided between the states and the central government.

But there were many areas of disagreement among the chosen delegates, some of which almost led to the Convention's dissolution. Each delegate was representing the best interests of his own state; and because the states had functioned much as separate nations, there were many areas where their values and goals would collide.

One major area of disagreement lay in the matter of how representation in the legislature would be figured. The larger states felt that a state's number of representatives should be determined by population. Their plan was proposed by Edmund Randolph of Virginia and was called the Virginia Plan. On the other side of the aisle were the states with fewer people who feared that the big states would control the government, so they insisted that all states have equal representation. Their plan was the idea of William Paterson and was called the New Jersey Plan. The conflict over which of these proposals would be adopted threatened to break up the Convention. Roger Sherman of Connecticut came forth at the point of disaster with a compromise that appeased both the larger states and the smaller states. His proposal called for a two-house legislature. There would be an upper house called the Senate in which each state would have equal representation. There would also be a lower house, the House of Representatives, in which each state would have one representative for every 30,000 inhabitants living in that state. Sherman's plan satisfied both the smaller states and the more populous states. It became historically known as the Connecticut Compromise or the Great Compromise.

Another area of great controversy lay in the manner of determining taxes. Taxes were to be based

John Rutledge

Oliver Ellsworth

Rufus King

John Dickinson

Edmund Randolph

Robert Morris

on the number of people in each state. For example, a larger state with twice as many people as a smaller state had to pay twice as much in taxes to support the national government. People living in the southern states did not want their slaves counted in the population because it would make their taxes higher as a result. They considered their slaves as property. But representation in the House of Representatives was based on population and the southern states wanted their slaves counted when it came to determining the number of representatives they would have. The delegates from the northern states felt just the opposite. Again the framers of the Constitution appeared to have reached a standoff with neither side willing to change its position.

Again compromise was the order of the day with a proposal brought forth called a *federal ratio* to solve the problem. In effect the proposal called for states to count three of every five slaves in their population, both for purposes of determining representation and taxation. The measure became known as the *three-fifths compromise.* The authors of the Constitution also carefully avoided using the word *slave* in the Constitution, but the issue constantly emerged because of the different economic concerns and values between the northern states and the southern slaveholding states.

On the issue of whether or not to allow slave trading, they finally settled the issue by allowing it to continue for twenty years through 1807—no doubt hoping that the issue would resolve itself by that time.

Finally, the delegates wrestled with the problem of how much power to give to the central government. They knew it had to be strong, because the Articles of Confederation had not provided for a strong central government and they had failed. But there needed to be some way to check and restrain the powers given to the central government to keep it from the potential abuses of unlimited powers. This they accomplished by having each of the three branches of government accountable to the other two. The Congress, for example, can make laws, but the President has the power to veto those he feels are not in the best interests of the nation. Congress can still override his veto, but the Supreme Court then has the power to rule out any law which they feel does not fall in line with the Constitution.

Because the delegates sent to the Convention didn't actually have the power to write a new Constitution, there was going to have to be approval from the states before it could become law. The Constitution itself provided for the rules of its ratification (Article 7). When the entire document was finished and signed, copies were dispatched to each of the states. Special conventions were then held in each of the states with the approval of nine states required to make the Constitution the law of the land. By the end of June in 1788, nine states had ratified the Constitution, but neither Virginia nor New York was among them. Everyone knew that without these two states the new Constitution would never work. Virginia/New York had not ratified the Constitution because many people in those states had objected to there not being much emphasis on individual rights in the new framework of government. Both states finally approved the Constitution with the condition that a number of amendments outlining specific rights and protection to individuals be added "at the earliest possible moment."

Both North Carolina and Rhode Island eventually approved the Constitution, but not until the new government was already in operation.

Congress did propose such a listing of human rights when it met in 1789 and by 1791 that list, known as the Bill of Rights, became a part of the Constitution in 1791.

Charles Pinckney

William Samuel Johnson

Name _____

Looking back at... the Background

1. What caused the historical incident referred to as ''Shays' Rebellion''? Why was it a sign of the times?

_____

_____

_____

_____

_____

2. The men who wrote the Constitution actually gathered together with the idea of merely revising the Articles of Confederation. But they found them to be so un-workable that they decided to start all over. List some of the more important reasons for the framers of the Constitution making the decision to write an entirely new framework of government.

_____

_____

_____

_____

_____

_____

_____

_____

3. One of the big questions faced by the Convention was the debate over the matter of representation in the Congress. Describe the controversy between the large states and the smaller states and the major provisions of the New Jersey and Virginia Plans. How was the issue finally resolved through compromise?

_____

_____

_____

_____

_____

_____

_____

_____

_____

_____

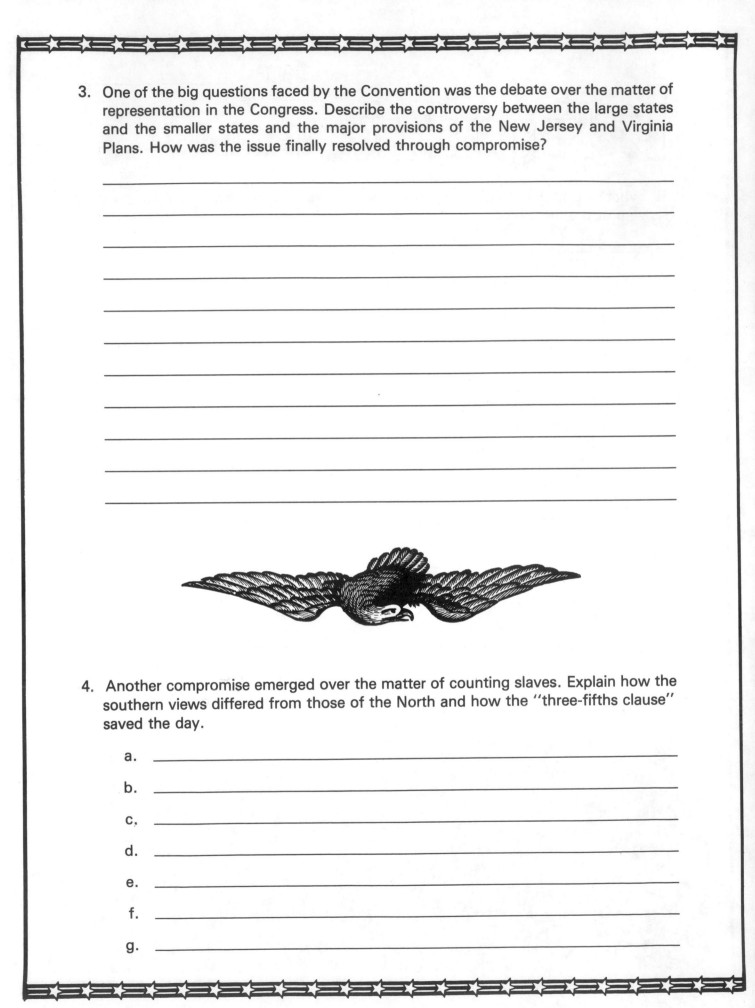

4. Another compromise emerged over the matter of counting slaves. Explain how the southern views differed from those of the North and how the "three-fifths clause" saved the day.

    a. _____

    b. _____

    c. _____

    d. _____

    e. _____

    f. _____

    g. _____

5. It has been said that the Constitution is ". . . the most wonderful work ever struck off at a given time by the brain and purpose of man." How can such a statement be made about a document that has already been changed (amended) twenty-six times?

_____

_____

_____

_____

_____

_____

_____

_____

6. Find evidence in what you read in the introduction that will help to explain this statement: "Those who control the power to govern are resistant to any kind of change because they fear such changes will decrease their power."

_____

_____

_____

_____

_____

7. Rhode Island was the only state not represented at the Constitutional Convention. Why did this tiny state refuse to send delegates to such an important and historical meeting?

_____

_____

_____

_____

_____

8. The delegates who came to the Constitutional Convention represented several different occupations. Among them were several lawyers, businessmen and southern planters. There were other occupations, but none of them were less than at least moderately successful financially. How do you account for the fact that none were what we could call "common men"?

_____

_____

_____

_____

_____

_____

_____

9. Why do you suppose the delegates decided soon after they convened to work behind closed doors?

_____

_____

_____

_____

_____

_____

_____

10. When we think of the U.S. Constitution, we usually think of the name of George Washington. Even though he was very important as president of the Convention, there were several other names we should remember as well. Below are the names of several of these leaders who were at the Philadelphia Convention. Choose any two and research the contribution made by each; then write an essay describing the contribution of each as well as developing a contrast between the two.

Oliver Ellsworth	William Paterson	Benjamin Franklin
Roger Sherman	Rufus King	Edmund Randolph
Robert Morris	John Rutledge	John Dickinson
George Wythe	William Samuel Johnson	Alexander Hamilton
James Madison	Gouverneur Morris	Charles Pinckney

Name _____

DRAWING CONCLUSIONS

Below are the results of the votes taken in each state by the special convention called to ratify the Constitution. Look closely at them and decide which of the conclusions can be called true and which cannot.

	State	Date	For Ratification	Against
1.	Delaware	Dec. 7, 1787	30	0
2.	Pennsylvania	Dec. 12, 1787	46	23
3.	New Jersey	Dec. 18, 1787	38	0
4.	Georgia	Jan. 2, 1788	26	0
5.	Connecticut	Jan. 9, 1788	128	40
6.	Massachusetts	Feb. 6, 1788	187	168
7.	Maryland	Apr. 28, 1788	63	11
8.	South Carolina	May 23, 1788	149	73
9.	New Hampshire	June 21, 1788	57	47
10.	Virginia	June 25, 1788	89	79
11.	New York	July 26, 1788	30	27
12.	North Carolina	Nov. 21, 1789	196	77
13.	Rhode Island	May 29, 1790	34	32

1. _____ The closest vote was in the state of New York.

2. _____ Conventions in all 13 states approved ratification of the Constitution.

3. _____ The southern states were more favorable toward ratification than the New England states.

4. _____ The states which ratified the Constitution earliest seemed to do so with overwhelming approval.

5. _____ Connecticut had the widest margin of votes in favor of ratification.

6. _____ Pennsylvania delegates approved of the Constitution by a vote of 2:1.

7. _____ The Constitution went into effect before all states had approved its ratification.

8. _____ The state with the most delegates was North Carolina.

9. _____ Three states ratified the Constitution unanimously.

10. _____ The big states were more in favor of the Constitution than the small states.

Draw three conclusions of your own from the voting results in the chart above that are different from those already stated.

_____

_____

_____

25

Name _____

PREAMBLE

The original Constitution contained seven articles. There have been twenty-six changes or additions to those seven articles. The changes are called amendments. The very first paragraph that precedes the actual text of the Constitution is called the Preamble. In it the men who wrote the Constitution summarize the reasons why it was written. We might better call it a *statement of purpose.*

We the people of the United States, in order to form a more perfect Union,	We the representatives of the American people are creating this Constitution for the following reasons:
establish justice,	We want a better, more efficient system of government than was possible under the Articles of Confederation.
ensure domestic tranquility,	We want all people treated fairly under the same laws.
provide for the common defense,	We want to ensure a peaceful existence within the United States.
promote the general welfare, and	We want to ensure an adequate defense against those who would be our enemies.
secure the blessings of liberty to ourselves and our posterity,	We want to encourage what is good for all the people.
do ordain and establish this Constitution for the United States of America.	We want to keep our freedom and make certain that our children and our children's children have those same freedoms.

Can you summarize in a paragraph the reasons why the Constitution was written? _____

_____

_____

_____

If a new Constitution were to be written today what reasons, other than those cited in

the Preamble, would you list as reasons for writing a constitution? _____

_____

_____

Name _____

PREAMBLE SCRAMBLE

Below is the Preamble to the Constitution of the United States. Your task is to find it in this jumble of letters. You may make only 90° turns, but you may move your pencil in any direction.

```
T W E T H E P E O P L E R V W I T E R P S R T O F D O M N U X Y M
O R M T H Z Q O P S O O I H M N T D S O K R A B C Z P E P F Q O R
E T I N U F O E H T F F T H E U O S T S O C P F E H R T O I R M V
P E R F E C T U S K T B A N R E L T A A B A K C A B F Y A N V A S
T E W O H A P N T M H A N A P U B A L S K O C D T U F B R E W Y M
R L T M T S M I A V E U N I T E D T U P N E I R F T S E B Y R E V
Q F S P Y B O O R O H L I T D O S E A T E S O F B E F R E I A N E
E S O S R U R N S I E A H W I N G S C O M E S A S T O T S A J R O
E R O M A M R O F O T R E D R O N I A C I R E M I H S I N E R G G
P R U S N I N N A T S E Z H T W Z I L A R O N M M E S T N I V R B
E R F E C T U T L I S H J U S T I C E I N O N E O L T I C A T I S
E D O M E S N E B W O N T H Y B F L D N S U R E D G C C T O T U O
L V Q C I T I V A F D N O M Y A R O O V A P A B A G N T O M H E I
I I N A R T O V T L S O P O M O R G F O R R H L T S E R F E D I D
T Y A F D N N E S O Y D O T M A P T H O F F S I T R Y A N Q U I L
S R T N A U S A I T S U P E P I E R E E O R T Y H E E A R S M A I
D E H O Y S T P S H T J E T E A S G N O M M O C E H T R O F D R T
A F L E W L A R E N E G E H N I N T D T E L H V S I T T R E N I Y
O A N C E M W E H I W M I H G T E F E N T B I A G N O S E D A O P
D R E H W I H N E R N T H E P O R L A D W T S D A D A T T I V O R
O E N V O I H T N A C H E L L P E D U H O I F Y A R P E Y F T Y H
U A N D H T E M N N G S O F O D D R N E K C I G D S R N I F A T E
T T V S S T I H T I N H I L B V T S E L V E S A N D A I T Y D O O
I J E E M T G P V S L H M I I T U R B T C M E N T O V R S I S A R
S U T C T H T U V S E T I B H H O U E T D U D H S U I E O N I T D
T J D U S V O P O E M H N E T G M O J R E L P R E R L T H T E C A
G E N R E T H E B L V M O R T Y T O V D A D N A R P O S E N R O I
E R A C O N S T I T U T I O N F O R T H H S I L B A T S E D N A N
E D L A R A S A C I V M O T S T I N V H T P V O A H E M A U T N E
F A N Y A S L G E L G I L O L M O S S O H I S C O N S T I T U T I
G R O A G T F O H O C N K D D O R F A F H T H O Y T N I C S D C O
N T U N D A C I R E M A F O S E T A T S D E T I N U E H T R O F N
C E I H A D F O T W E N T O S T O L L C C S T R I N G J S A T O U
```

☆ ARTICLE I—LEGISLATIVE DEPARTMENT ☆

Article 1 clearly points out the powers and restrictions of the legislative or lawmaking branch of our government. Several changes have been made to Article 1 since it was written, but it is important to study the original text first to better understand why it was necessary for those changes.

Article 1, Section 1. All *legislative* powers herein granted shall be vested in a *Congress* of the United States, which shall consist of a *Senate* and *House of Representatives.*

Article 1, Section 2, clause 1. The House of Representatives shall be composed of members chosen every second year by the people of the several states, and the electors in each state shall have the qualifications requisite for electors of the most numerous branch of the state legislature.

Article 1, Section 2, clause 2. No person shall be a representative who shall not have attained to the age of twenty-five years, and been seven years a citizen of the United States, and who shall not, when elected, be an inhabitant of that state in which he shall be chosen.

Power Defined

The power to make laws that govern the people of the United States is given to Congress. Congress is made up of two separate houses; one is called the U.S. Senate, the other is the House of Representatives.

House of Representatives

Members of the House of Representatives are chosen by voters of the states they represent every two years. People who are allowed to vote for their own state lawmakers shall also be eligible to vote for the representatives of the House. *Many states formerly had restrictions on who could vote. Amendments to the Constitution have lifted those restrictions.*

Qualifications

To become a member of the U.S. House of Representatives, one must be:
1. 25 years of age
2. a U.S. citizen for at least seven years
3. live in the state from which he is chosen

Since the Constitution was written, most states have been divided into districts—each district being allowed one representative. Candidates must live in the districts they intend to serve.

Article 1, Section 2, clause 3. Representatives and direct taxes shall be *apportioned* among the several states which may be included within this Union, according to their respective numbers, which shall be determined by adding to the whole number of free persons, including those bound to service for a term of years, and excluding Indians not taxed, three-fifths of all *other persons.*

The actual enumeration shall be made within three years after the first meeting of the Congress of the United States, and within every subsequent term of ten years, in such manner as they shall by law direct.

The number of representatives shall not exceed one for every thirty thousand, but each state shall have at least one representative; and until such enumeration shall be made, the state of New Hampshire shall be entitled to choose three, Massachusetts eight, Rhode Island and Providence Plantations one, Connecticut five, New York six, New Jersey four, Pennsylvania eight, Delaware one, Maryland six, Virginia ten, North Carolina five, South Carolina five, and Georgia three.

Article 1, Section 2, clause 4. When vacancies happen in the representation from any state, the executive authority thereof shall issue writs of election to fill such vacancies.

Article 1, Section 2, clause 5. The House of Representatives shall choose their *speaker* and other officers;

Representation

The number of representatives each state is allowed is determined by the population of that state. *Two parts of this clause no longer apply. Direct taxes are no longer based on population, but rather income (16th Amendment). Also the 13th Amendment nullified the three-fifths clause because it outlawed slavery.*

A census or count of the people is authorized by Congress every ten years beginning with the first year of the decade.

The number of representatives for each state was originally based on 30,000 persons per representative. Because the population has grown a great deal, there are now many more than 30,000 persons represented by each representative. But the proportion remains the same. That is, each congressional district has about the same number of persons. In 1910 the number of representatives was frozen at 435.

Filling Vacancies

When a representative dies or resigns his office, the governor of the state he represents calls for a special election to fill the vacancy.

Organization

The House of Representatives elects its own officers. Its leader is called the speaker. *Each Congress lasts for two years. The speaker or chosen leader is the most powerful member of the House of Representatives.*

and shall have the sole power of impeachment.

Article 1, Section 3, clause 1. The Senate of the United States shall be composed of two *senators* from each state, chosen by the *legislature* thereof; for six years; and each senator shall have one vote.

Article 1, Section 3, clause 2. Immediately after they shall be assembled in consequence of the first election, they shall be divided as equally as may be into three classes. The seats of the senators of the first class shall be vacated at the expiration of the second year, of the second class at the expiration of the fourth year, and of the third class at the expiration of the sixth year, so that one-third may be chosen every second year; and if vacancies happen by resignation, or otherwise, during the recess of the legislature of any state, the executive thereof may make temporary appointments until the next meeting of the legislature, which shall then fill such vacancies.

Article 1, Section 3, clause 3. No person shall be a senator who shall not have attained to the age of thirty years, and been nine years a citizen of the United States, and who shall not, when elected, be an inhabitant of that state for which he shall be chosen.

Impeachment

Only the House of Representatives has the power to impeach. The power of impeachment is defined as the power to determine whether or not high officials in the executive and judicial department should be formally accused of doing something so bad while in office that they should no longer be allowed to serve in the public trust. (Note: They do not conduct the actual trial. They merely file the formal accusation which means they will face a trial in the U.S. Senate. It is there that the guilt or innocence is determined. The House of Representatives stands as the accuser.)

U.S. Senators

The Senate Chamber has two senators from each state. Senators were chosen by the state legislatures under the original Constitution. The 17th Amendment changed that so they are now elected by the people. Senators serve six-year terms and each has one vote.

Terms of Office Are Staggered

The terms of U.S. senators are arranged so that one-third of the senators are elected every two years. The first time Congress met, one-third were elected for two-year terms; one-third were elected for four-year terms and one-third elected for six-year terms. Thereafter all senators would serve six-year terms of office. The reason for this arrangement is so that the entire Senate is never elected in a single election.

Qualifications for Office

To become a U.S. senator, one must be thirty years old, a U.S. citizen for nine years and live in the state he or she represents.

Article 1, Section 3, clause 4. The Vice-President of the United States shall be president of the Senate, but shall have no vote, unless they be equally divided.

Article 1, Section 3, clause 5. The Senate shall choose their other officers, and also a president pro tempore, in the absence of the Vice-President, or when he shall exercise the Office of President of the United States.

Article 1, Section 3, clause 6. The Senate shall have the sole power to try all *impeachments.* When sitting for that purpose, they shall be on *oath* or *affirmation.* When the President of the United States is tried, the *Chief Justice* shall preside; and no person shall be convicted without the concurrence of two-thirds of the members present.

Article 1, Section 3, clause 7. Judgment in cases of impeachment shall not extend further than to removal from office and disqualification to hold and enjoy any office of honor, trust, or profit under the United States; but the party convicted shall nevertheless be liable and subject to indictment, trial, judgment and punishment, according to law.

Senate Organization

The Vice-President of the United States presides over all meetings of the U.S. Senate and votes only when there is a tie.

Other Offices

The Senate chooses its other officers, including a *president pro tempore,* who will preside over the Senate when the Vice-President is unable to attend because of his duties as Vice-President.

Trying Impeachments

The Senate has the sole power to try those who have been impeached by members of the House of Representatives. The entire Senate serves as the jury and they take an oath that promises to try the accused fairly. If it is the President on trial, then the Chief Justice of the Supreme Court presides over the trial. Otherwise, the Vice-President presides. To convict the accused requires a two-thirds vote of all members present.

Extent of Punishment

In cases where the Senate finds the accused guilty, their power is limited to removing the official from office and preventing him from holding another office. But the convicted official can nevertheless be tried in a regular court of law, and if found guilty, could be punished according to the laws.

Looking back at... Membership in Congress

Article I, Sections 1-3

1. What is the main content focus of Article 1? _____
   _____

2. In a single sentence, describe the main function of the legislative department. ____
   _____
   _____

3. The lawmaking branch of our government consists of two houses or chambers.
   They are _____
   _____

4. The two houses together are called _____

Qualifications for Membership

	House	Senate
5. Minimum Age Requirement:	_____	_____
Citizenship Requirement:	_____	_____
Residential Requirement:	_____	_____
Term of Office:	_____	_____
Number of Members:	_____	_____

6. What is the title of the main officer in the U.S. House of Representatives? _____
   _____

   That office is currently filled by _____

7. Who presides over the U.S. Senate? _____

   Who presently holds that office? _____

8. What is the sole factor in determining the number of representatives each state is entitled to have in the U.S. House of Representatives? _____

_____

Who is your Congressman? _____

How many representatives does your state have? _____

What congressional district do you live in? _____

Each state has two U.S. senators. Who are your U.S. senators?

_____

_____

9. What happens in the event of a vacancy occurring in either chamber of Congress?

_____

_____

10. Explain why the framers of the Constitution felt it necessary to have a legislature composed of two houses. _____

_____

_____

11. Which house of Congress would have been favored by the smaller states?
_____ Why? _____

_____

12. Which house would have been favored by the larger more populous states?
_____ Why? _____

_____

Impeachment

13. What is the purpose of impeachment? _____

_____

_____

Why was it made a part of the Constitution? _____

_____

_____

Why was the power given to Congress and what is the role played by each house in the impeachment process? _____

_____

_____

House's Role: _____   Senate's Role: _____

_____   _____

_____   _____

_____   _____

14. What vote is necessary in the House to achieve an impeachment? _____

_____

What vote is necessary in the Senate to get a conviction? _____

_____

15. Which President was impeached? _____

16. What was the nature of his alleged wrongdoing? _____

_____

_____

What was the result of his trial in the Senate? _____

_____

17. Why would it be appropriate for the Chief Justice of the Supreme Court to preside over an impeachment trial of a President? _____

_____

18. In more recent times, President Richard Nixon was "almost impeached." What was the nature of his alledged wrongdoing and how did he escape impeachment? _____

_____

19. Each house of Congress has some important leaders who have a great deal of power and importance in controlling party politics within their respective chambers. Find out the current name of each and indicate his party affiliation with D for Democrat and R for Republican.

House of Representatives

Speaker _____

Majority Leader _____

Majority Whip _____

Minority Leader _____

Minority Whip _____

Senate

Vice-President _____

president pro tempore _____

Majority Whip _____

Minority Leader _____

Minority Whip _____

20. All meetings of Congress are identified by a number. What number is currently in session? _____

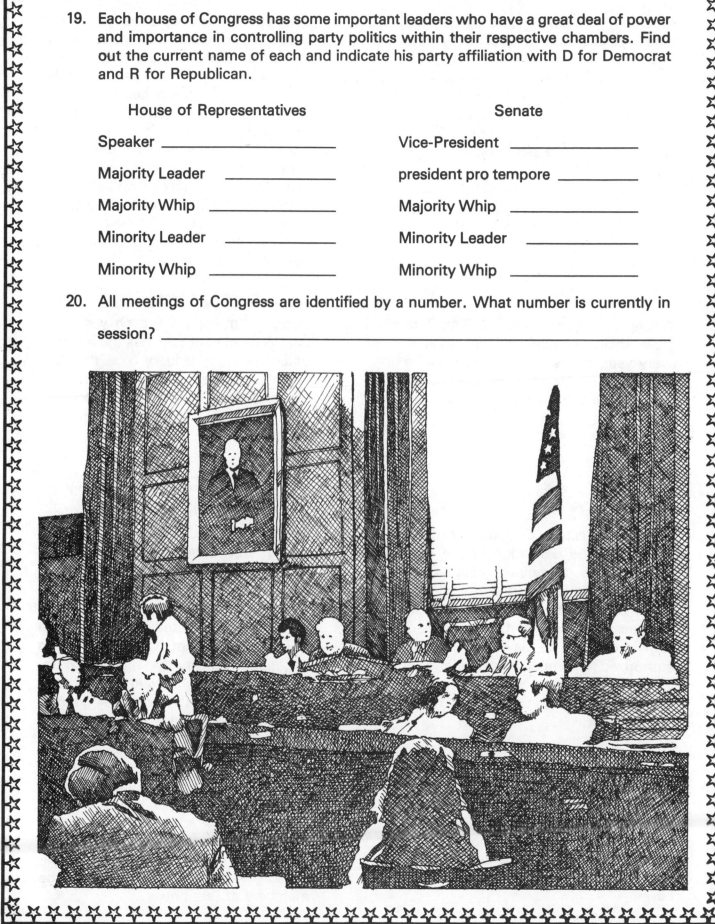

Article 1, Section 4, clause 1. The times, places, and manner of holding elections for senators and representatives shall be prescribed in each state by the legislature thereof; but the Congress may at any time by law make or alter such regulations, except as to the places of choosing senators.

Article 1, Section 4, clause 2. The Congress shall assemble at least once in every year, and such meeting shall be on the first Monday in December, unless they shall by law appoint a different day.

Article 1, Section 5, clause 1. Each house shall be the judge of the elections, returns, and qualifications of its own members, and a majority of each shall constitute a *quorum* to do business; but a smaller number may *adjourn* from day to day, and may be authorized to compel the attendance of absent members, in such manner, and under such penalties as each house may provide.

Article 1, Section 5, clause 2. Each house may determine the rules of its proceedings, punish its members for disorderly behavior, and, with the concurrence of two-thirds, expel a member.

Election

All matters regarding times, places and procedures of election are controlled by the state. But Congress can overrule any such state rule and establish rules of its own. Congress has determined that its members shall be elected on the Tuesday after the first Monday in November in all even-numbered years. This is called a *general election*. All elections are done by secret ballot. The 17th Amendment overrules the last part of the last sentence of clause 1—U.S. senators are now elected by the people just as representatives.

When Congress Meets

Congress meets once each year. The 20th Amendment changes the last part of clause 2 to January 3 as the date when Congress meets each year. With the exception of weekends, recesses and vacations, the meeting lasts most of the year.

Qualifications of Membership and Quorum Defined

In the case of a disputed election, each house can determine if its elected members are suitable and desirable. Even though a person has been duly elected by the people, the house to which he was elected has the right to refuse to seat him if it feels he has engaged in activity that makes him unworthy of the honor. Neither house can meet unless it has a *quorum*. A quorum is defined as more than half the members present.

Membership Conduct

Each house shall make its own rules for conducting its affairs and punish its members who may break the rules. A member of either house may be expelled by a two-thirds vote of the members of that house.

Article 1, Section 5, clause 3. Each house shall keep a *journal* of its proceedings, and from time to time publish the same, excepting such parts as may in their judgment require secrecy; and the yeas and nays of the members of either house on any question shall, at the desire of one-fifth of those present, be entered on the journal.

Article 1, Section 5, clause 4. Neither house, during the session of Congress, shall, without the consent of the other, *adjourn* for more than three days, nor to any other place than that in which the two houses shall be sitting.

Article 1, Section 6, clause 1. The senators and representatives shall receive a *compensation* for their services, to be ascertained by law, and paid out of the treasury of the United States.

They shall in all cases, except *treason, felony* and *breach of the peace,* be privileged from arrest during their attendance at the session of their respective houses, and in going to and returning from the same; and for any speech or debate in either house, they shall not be questioned in any other place.

Congressional Record

Both the House and the Senate keep records of what is said and done each day it meets. Certain proceedings can be kept secret if the membership desires, but a request by one-fifth of the members present can force all voting to be made public knowledge. In practice every word that is said plus all legislation considered each day in Congress is published at the end of each day in the *Congressional Record.* Included are the results of all votes taken and how each member voted.

Congress in Recess

During sessions of Congress, neither house can recess for more than three days without agreement from both houses. Both houses must also meet in the same city. *The purpose of this clause is to allow members of Congress to do their work without interference from those who might make meeting difficult through time and place restrictions and red tape. The city in which they meet is Washington, D.C.*

Membership Privileges

Members of Congress shall receive an annual salary paid out of the United States Treasury according to laws which they themselves establish. Members also enjoy freedom from arrest except for treason and serious crimes while meetings are in session. Also members can say what they want during all meetings, as nothing they may say can be held against them. *This paragraph was built into the Constitution to prevent those who would detain or prevent members of Congress from meeting to vote on key issues.*

Article 1, Section 6, clause 2. No senator or representative shall, during the time for which he was elected, be appointed to any civil office under the authority of the United States which shall have been created, or the *emoluments* whereof shall have been increased during such time; and no person holding any office under the United States shall be a member of either house during his continuance in office.

Membership Restrictions

Members of Congress cannot hold any other government offices or jobs while in office; nor can they resign while in office and take another job that was created while they were in office; nor can they take jobs for which the salary was increased while they were in office.

Looking back on... Article I, Sections 4-6

Name _____

1. What is the rule Congress has established for the election of its membership?

   _____

   _____

2. On what date will the next general election be held? (Hint: You may need to find a perpetual calendar in an almanac to answer this one.)

   _____

3. On what date does Congress normally begin its annual meeting unless otherwise determined?

   _____

4. What do you think is the reason for voting booths and all the security associated with the secret ballot system we use here in the United States?

   _____

   _____

5. How is a quorum defined in Article 1, Section 5, as it applies to Congress?

   _____

   How many members constitute a quorum in each house? _____House of Representatives, _____ Senate

6. Each house is responsible for the conduct of its own members. What vote is required by either house to expel a member of that house? _____

   How many representatives would be required to expel a member of the House? _____ How many senators would be required to expel a senator from the Senate? _____

7. Do you think it's fair that the people of a congressional district might elect a candidate—then have the House of Representatives vote not to seat that person? Before you answer, think of the reason why the framers of the Constitution made this rule a part of the Constitution.

_____

_____

_____

8. What fraction of either house of Congress is necessary to require voting in that house to be made public knowledge?

_____

9. In this nation of voting booths and secret ballots, why is it appropriate for members of Congress to make it a matter of public knowledge the way they vote on laws and issues brought before Congress?

_____

10. The official minutes of Congress are published daily whenever Congress is in session. What is this official record called?

_____

Have your teacher obtain a recent copy for your class and note the interesting events that occurred in Congress on that particular day.

11. What is the longest recess one house can take without the consent of the other?

_____

12. Can you think of reasons why Article 1, Section 5, clause 4 provides that both houses must be in session at the same time?

_____

_____

_____

13. Find out the annual salary of members of Congress. Since members of Congress establish their own salaries, what would prevent them from voting themselves larger pay raises?

_____

_____

14. Find out the theory behind granting members of Congress freedom from arrest while Congress is in session except for serious crimes.

_____

_____

_____

15. Look again at Article 1, Section 6, clause 2. What would be wrong with having a member of Congress resign his office to take a newly created position in government if in fact he is well-qualified to fill that position?

_____

_____

Name _____

Dear Congressman...

The members of both houses of Congress are there to serve us. After all, we are the reasons they have their jobs. It is thus their duty to serve our needs and see that our interests are protected. They do this by initiating laws and voting on laws that will be of help to us. They also should vote against laws that would not be good for us. A law that might benefit people in New York City might be bad for people living in Cheyenne, Wyoming. When an important law is being debated and is due for a vote, it is often helpful for these congressmen to hear from the people they serve. Find out how to write to your congressmen and U.S. senators and list their mailing addresses below:

_____   _____   _____
_____   _____   _____
_____   _____   _____
_____   _____   _____

In the space that follows, write a letter to one of them explaining your position on a current issue of concern to you.

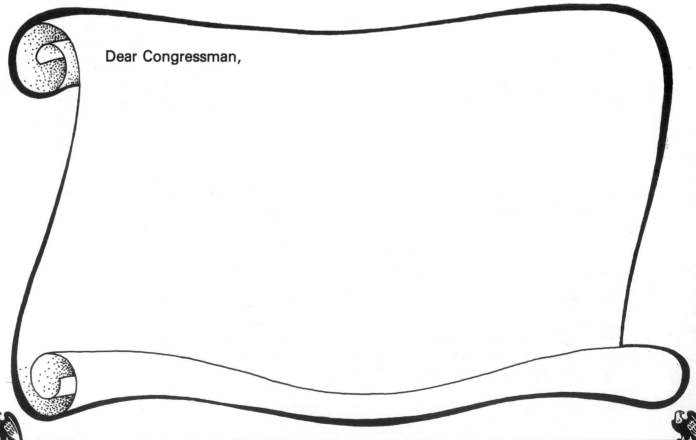

Dear Congressman,

Article 1, Section 7, clause 1. All *bills* for raising revenue shall originate in the House of Representatives; but the Senate may propose or concur with amendments as on other bills.

Article 1, Section 7, clause 2. Every bill which shall have passed the House of Representatives and the Senate, shall, before it becomes a law, be presented to the President of the United States. If he approves, he shall sign it, but if not he shall return it, with his objections, to that house in which it shall have originated, who shall enter the objections at large on their journal, and proceed to reconsider it. If after such reconsideration two-thirds of that house shall agree to pass the bill, it shall be sent, together with the objections, to the other house, by which it shall likewise be reconsidered, and if approved by two-thirds of that house, it shall become a law. But in all such cases the votes of both houses shall be determined by yeas and nays, and the names of the persons voting for and against the bill shall be entered on the journal of each house respectively.

Revenue Bills

All bills involving the increasing of taxes to raise money must begin in the House of Representatives, but Senate approval is necessary for the bill to become a law. The Senate may also propose changes or amendments as it does on other bills.

The reason only the House has this power to initiate revenue bills goes back to the original Constitution in which only House members were elected by the people. Senators were chosen by the state legislatures and the writers of the Constitution did not want laws involving money started by men who had not been elected by the people.

Presidential Veto

Once a bill has successfully been approved by both the House and the Senate, it is sent on to the President for his approval. If he approves, he signs it and the bill will become a law. If he does not approve, he returns it unsigned to the house where it originated along with his objection. If that house wishes to keep the bill just as it was, then two-thirds of the members present must vote in its favor. If this happens, the bill is then sent on to the other house. If two-thirds of the members present favor the bill, then the bill will become a law despite the President's veto.

Failure of President to Act on Bill

The President has ten days (not counting Sundays) to act on legislation once he has been sent a bill approved by Congress. If he fails to sign or veto the bill within that time, then the bill becomes a law without his signature. If Congress adjourns during this time, then the President doesn't have to act on the bill because it won't become a law if he fails to sign it. Such failure to act by the President is called a pocket veto.

Congress passes many bills daily that do not affect the general public. For lack of time the President often does nothing about these bills, because he knows that the unsigned bills will become laws anyway.

Orders and Resolutions of Congress

Any other orders, resolutions or votes by Congress (except the matter of adjournment) require the President's approval. If the President vetoes the action by Congress, it takes a two-thirds vote of both houses of Congress to override his veto.

Article 1, Section 7, clause 3. Every *order, resolution,* or vote to which the concurrence of the Senate and House of Representatives may be necessary (except on a question of adjournment) shall be presented to the President of the United States; and before the same shall take effect, shall be approved by him, or being disapproved by him, shall be repassed by two-thirds of the Senate and House of Representatives, according to the rules and limitations prescribed in the case of a bill.

A bill can start in either house of Congress. Only bills dealing with revenue must start in the House of Representatives. If a proposed law (bill) fails to achieve the required approval anywhere along the way, the bill dies. To become a law, it must follow one of the routes outlined below.

A bill may begin in the mind of anyone—even the President—but it must be presented before Congress by a member of Congress.

He presents his idea to his staff, and the rough idea is refined into a proposed bill.

The bill is then sent to its appropriate committee where it is studied. Hearings are held and evidence gathered to decide if the bill has merit. The committee can add or delete as it sees fit.

The committee then votes. If the committee approves, the bill goes before the full House or Senate (depending on where the bill was initiated).

The proper committee receives the bill and studies the bill much the same as the committee in the other house did.

Once all the evidence is in and any changes are made, the committee votes. If it approves, the bill is brought before the full house of Congress.

That first house then considers any changes that were made. If it approves of all the changes, the bill is sent on to the President.

If this house where the bill originated feels some compromise is in order, a committee from both houses rewrites certain parts of the bill.

If the President signs the bill, it becomes the law of the land.

If the President does not approve, he vetoes the bill and it is returned to the house where it originated.

Teacher Note: Pages 43 and 44 show how a bill becomes a law. Reproduce both pages and have students tape them together for their study of the route followed.

43

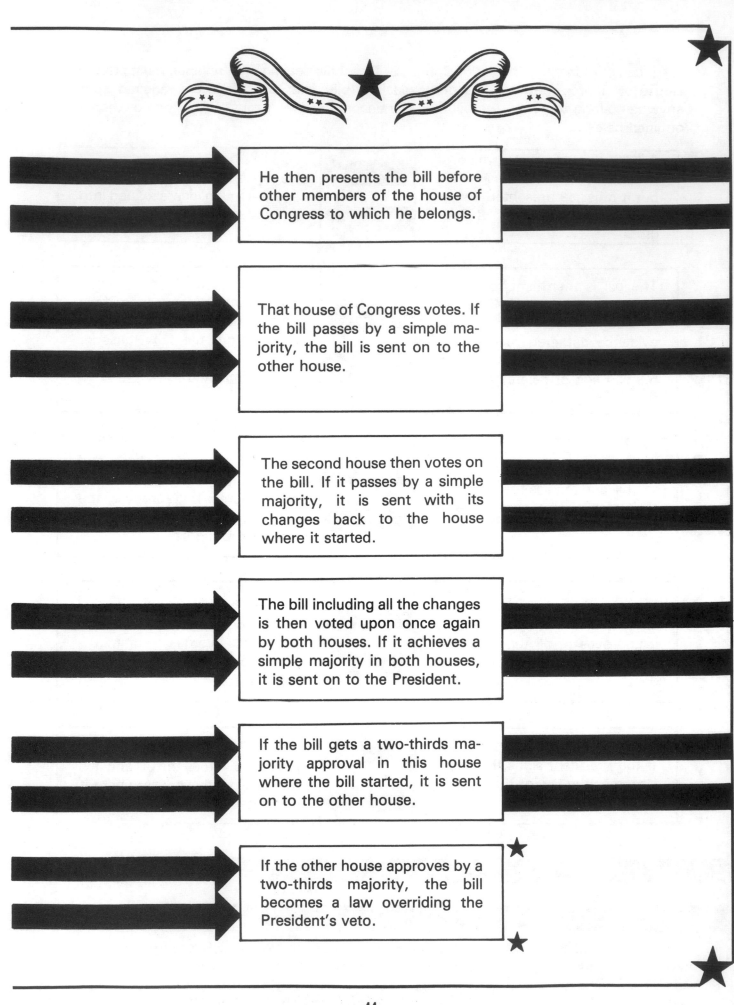

He then presents the bill before other members of the house of Congress to which he belongs.

That house of Congress votes. If the bill passes by a simple majority, the bill is sent on to the other house.

The second house then votes on the bill. If it passes by a simple majority, it is sent with its changes back to the house where it started.

The bill including all the changes is then voted upon once again by both houses. If it achieves a simple majority in both houses, it is sent on to the President.

If the bill gets a two-thirds majority approval in this house where the bill started, it is sent on to the other house.

If the other house approves by a two-thirds majority, the bill becomes a law overriding the President's veto.

CHARTING HB-1117

After studying the chart showing the various steps necessary for a bill to become a law, briefly summarize these steps in your own words so that you will remember them. You may build a chart of your own—or you may merely list the steps.

Build a flow chart showing the path followed by HB-1117, which eventually becomes a law despite the President's veto.

Summary of steps in how a bill becomes a law:

Flow chart for HB-1117

Name _____

EXPRESSING DISAPPROVAL

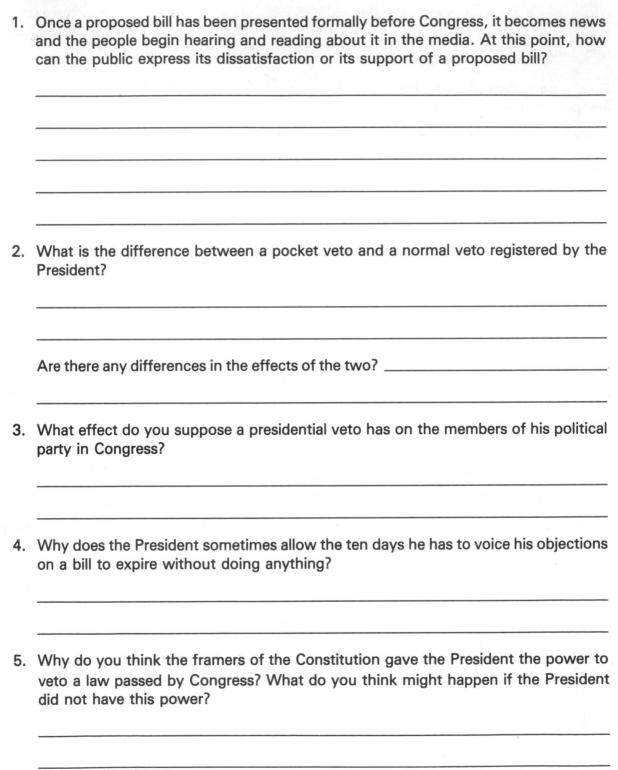

1. Once a proposed bill has been presented formally before Congress, it becomes news and the people begin hearing and reading about it in the media. At this point, how can the public express its dissatisfaction or its support of a proposed bill?

   _____

   _____

   _____

   _____

   _____

2. What is the difference between a pocket veto and a normal veto registered by the President?

   _____

   _____

   Are there any differences in the effects of the two? _____

   _____

3. What effect do you suppose a presidential veto has on the members of his political party in Congress?

   _____

   _____

4. Why does the President sometimes allow the ten days he has to voice his objections on a bill to expire without doing anything?

   _____

   _____

5. Why do you think the framers of the Constitution gave the President the power to veto a law passed by Congress? What do you think might happen if the President did not have this power?

   _____

   _____

Express Powers of Congress

Article 1, Section 8, clause 1. The Congress shall have power to *lay* and collect *taxes, duties, imposts,* and *excises* to pay the debts and provide for the common defense and general welfare of the United States; but all duties, imposts, and excises shall be uniform throughout the United States;

Congress has the power to collect taxes to pay debts, provide for an adequate defense and provide services for the good of all the people. All duties on imports and excise taxes must be the same throughout the country.

Article 1, Section 8, clause 2. To borrow money on the credit of the United States;

Congress has the power to borrow money.

Article 1, Section 8, clause 3. To regulate *commerce* with foreign nations, and among the several states, and with the Indian tribes;

Congress has the power to regulate trade, both foreign and domestic. *Domestic trade is defined as trade among states within the United States.*

Article 1, Section 8, clause 4. To establish a uniform rule of *naturalization,* and uniform laws on the subject of *bankruptcies* throughout the United States;

Congress establishes rules on foreign-born persons becoming citizens of the United States. Congress also makes the rules regarding bankruptcies. *Naturalization is defined as making a foreign-born person a citizen of the United States.* Bankruptcy occurs when a person builds his debts to a point far beyond his ability to pay them. When this happens, the courts take his property and split it up among his creditors.

Article 1, Section 8, clause 5. To coin money, regulate the value thereof, and of foreign coin, and fix the standard of weights and measures;

Congress has the power to coin money, establish its worth and determine the value of foreign money in U.S. dollars. Congress also sets the standards for weights and measures within the United States.

Article 1, Section 8, clause 6. To provide for the punishment of counterfeiting the securities and current coin of the United States;

Congress has the power to punish those who counterfeit U.S. money and bonds. *Counterfeit is defined as making fake money or U.S. bonds.*

Article 1, Section 8, clause 7. To establish post offices and post roads;

Congress establishes all U.S. post offices and highways.

Article 1, Section 8, clause 8. To promote the progress of science and useful arts, by securing for limited times to authors and inventors the exclusive rights to their respective writings and discoveries;

Congress promotes the progress of science and the arts by passing patent and copyright laws that will protect the inventors/authors from being copied by others. *Patents are issued to inventors to protect their inventions; copyrights are issued to authors and composers who write books and music.*

Article 1, Section 8, clause 9. To constitute tribunals inferior to the Supreme Court;

Congress has the power to establish courts beneath the Supreme Court as needed.

Article 1, Section 8, clause 10. To define and punish piracies and felonies committed on the high seas, and offenses against the law of nations;

Congress has the power to make laws and punish those who break those laws on all U.S. waters. Also Congress can punish those who break international laws on our waters.

Article 1, Section 8, clause 11. To declare war, grant *letters of marque and reprisal,* and make rules concerning captures on land and water;

Congress has the power to declare war and make rules concerning the seizure of enemy property. *Letters of marque were permission granted to private persons to allow them to capture enemy ships in exchange for being allowed to keep the captured cargo. It was later agreed by international law for nations to stop this practice of encouraging legalized piracy.*

Article 1, Section 8, clause 12. To raise and support armies, but no *appropriation* of money to that use shall be for a longer term than two years;

Congress has the power to raise and support an army, but no money may be appropriated for its support for more than two years at a time.

Article 1, Section 8, clause 13. To provide and maintain a navy;

Congress has the power to raise and support a navy.

Article 1, Section 8, clause 14. To make rules for the government and regulation of the land and naval forces;

Congress has the power to make rules that regulate and control its army and navy.

Article 1, Section 8, clause 15. To provide for calling forth the *militia* to execute the laws of the Union, suppress insurrections and repel invasions;

Congress has the power to call forth state militia to help enforce the law, to quiet any riots and violence and to drive out invaders. *In practice these state militias, called the National Guard, are most often used to help in times of natural disasters—floods, tornadoes, hurricanes, etc.*

Article 1, Section 8, clause 16. To provide for organizing, arming, and disciplining the militia, and for governing such part of them as may be employed in the service of the United States, reserving to the states respectively the appointment of the officers and the authority of training the militia according to the discipline prescribed by Congress;

Congress has the power to provide for the organizing, training and disciplining of the soldiers in that state militia. But the states have the power to choose the officers of their National Guards and to train them according to the rules established by Congress.

Article 1, Section 8, clause 17. To exercise exclusive legislation in all cases whatsoever, over such district (not exceeding ten miles square) as may, by cession of particular states, and the acceptance of Congress, become the seat of the government of the United States, and to exercise like authority over all places purchased by the consent of the legislature of the state in which the same shall be, for the erection of forts, magazines, arsenals, dock-yards, and other needful buildings;

Congress has the power to make all the laws for the national capital (Washington, D.C.). That district to be governed is not to exceed 10 miles square. Congress shall exercise power over all places bought from the states for use as forts, arsenals, navy yards and public buildings. *The framers of the Constitution did not want the national capital to be in any state. As a result Virginia and Maryland gave up land where the two came together to form this district, later becoming the present-day seat of our national government—Washington, D.C.*

Name _____

EXPRESS POWERS OF CONGRESS

Tell which clause of Section 8 gives Congress the power to act in each of the following situations:

1. _____ establish a post office in Ferris, Illinois

2. _____ issue a patent to Kent Hamilton to protect the design of his new solar collector

3. _____ set the minimum prison sentence for those found guilty of counterfeiting U.S. currency

4. _____ authorize a new issue of government bonds

5. _____ determine the rules governing Carlo Ferraro's request for U.S. citizenship

6. _____ raise the tax on imported foreign cars to help stimulate the American automobile industry

7. _____ fix the penalties for those found guilty of violating laws on our high seas

8. _____ call out the National Guard units in Louisiana to restore law and order following recent riots associated with racial unrest

9. _____ declare war on a foreign nation that has attacked the United States

10. _____ authorize spending money to keep active a fleet of warships ready to defend the United States

11. _____ determine the city sales tax on purchases made in the city of Washington, D.C.

12. _____ authorize positions for ten more federal district judges

13. _____ establish 18 as the minimum age for the army and navy

14. _____ establish a set of rules for training members of the National Guard

15. _____ authorize next year's defense budget

16. _____ arrange for the Soviet Union to buy 20 million metric tons of wheat from American farmers

17. _____ authorize the issuing of a $2.00 coin

IMPLIED POWER

These first seventeen clauses of Section 8 point specifically to powers the framers of the Constitution felt Congress should have. They are referred to as the *express* powers of Congress. But the men who wrote the Constitution were smart enough to realize that as time moved on, there would be other matters and areas of concern emerge which should be ruled on by Congress. Thus they placed this last paragraph in Section 8 which has become known as the "elastic clause." It gives Congress implied power to act in other areas not specifically cited in the first 17 clauses and has had the effect of providing a great deal of additional strength for Congress.

Article 1, Section 8, clause 18. And to make all laws which shall be necessary and proper for carrying into execution the foregoing powers, and all other powers vested by this Constitution in the government of the United States, or in any department or officer thereof.

Congress shall have the power to make all laws necessary to enforce the powers granted it in the first 17 clauses. It shall also make laws needed to carry out powers granted to the government by this Constitution. *Congress must still work within the powers of the Constitution. It cannot simply make any laws it desires. There are also checks against this power through the veto of the President and the ability of the Supreme Court to rule laws unconstitutional which fall outside the framework of the Constitution.*

In the space below cite several examples in today's world where Congress has exercised implied power. Look in newspapers and magazines for additional ideas.

_____

_____

_____

_____

_____

_____

List some powers you feel Congress should have that are not listed in Article 1, Section 8.

_____

_____

_____

_____

"EXPRESS VS. IMPLIED" POWER

Pair up with a partner and together prepare an answer for each of the questions below.

1. Explain the difference between the *express* and *implied* powers contained in Section 8, and provide examples to support the strength clause 18 gives to Congress.

   _____

   _____

   _____

   _____

2. Article 1, Section 8, clause 2 gives Congress the power to borrow money. How does it go about borrowing this money? Also find out the present staggering national debt faced by our government.

   _____

   _____

   _____

   _____

3. Find out the present requirements that must be satisfied when a foreigner becomes

   a naturalized U.S. citizen. _____

   _____

   _____

   _____

4. What is the difference between patents and copyrights? _____

   _____

   _____

   What purpose do they serve? _____

   _____

Cite ten realistic examples of Section 8 that come from our everyday living. Place each on a separate slip of paper. On the reverse side tell whether your example is one of Congress exercising an *express* power or an *implied* power. When you are finished, exchange your choices with another team and try to figure out their answers as they do yours.

Prohibitions on Congress

Article 1, Section 9, clause 1. The migration or importation of such persons as any of the states now existing shall think proper to admit, shall not be prohibited by the Congress prior to the year one thousand eight hundred and eight, but a tax or duty may be imposed on such importation, not exceeding ten dollars for each person.

Prior to 1808, Congress could make no law forbidding slave trade. It could, however, impose a tax of $10 per slave on those brought into this country. *This clause was a part of the original compromise that led to agreement on the Constitution. Those who favored it and did not want control accepted the twenty-year delay. Those who were against slave trading avoided the issue by delaying it for twenty years.*

Article 1, Section 9, clause 2. The privilege of the writ of habeas corpus shall not be suspended, unless when in cases of rebellion or invasion the public safety may require it.

Writs of habeas corpus can only be suspended when the nation is in rebellion or being invaded by a foreign nation. *A writ of habeas corpus is a court order ordering that a person accused of committing a crime be brought before the court to determine if he is being legally detained.*

Article 1, Section 9, clause 3. No bill of attainder or ex post facto law shall be passed.

Congress cannot pass bills of attainder (laws made to punish particular individuals) nor ex post facto laws (making it illegal to have done something that was not against the law when it was done). *These kinds of things had been done by King George to jail those in the colonies who caused him trouble, and the framers of the Constitution wanted to outlaw it from ever happening again.*

Article 1, Section 9, clause 4. No capitation, or other direct tax shall be laid, unless in proportion to the census or enumeration herein before directed to be taken.

All taxes levied by Congress must be the same for all people living in the United States. Other direct taxes shall be based on population. *The 16th Amendment modified a part of this clause by making it legal to tax individuals according to their wealth (income tax).*

Article 1, Section 9, clause 5. No tax or duty shall be laid on articles exported from any state.

Congress shall not tax goods exported from any state.

Article 1, Section 9, clause 6. No preference shall be given by any regulation of commerce or revenue to the ports of one state over those of another; nor shall vessels bound to, or from, one state, be obliged to enter, clear, or pay duties in another.

Congress cannot pass laws that show preference of one state over another. Ships may travel on the waters of other states without paying duties. *This clause was put in the Constitution to avoid the quarrels that developed under the Articles of Confederation which allowed each state to make its own trade laws. Under that arrangement states began to charge unfair rates that often made the shipping charges cost more than the goods were worth.*

Article 1, Section 9, clause 7. No money shall be drawn from the treasury, but in consequence of appropriations made by law; and a regular statement and account of the receipts and expenditures of all public money shall be published from time to time.

No money can be drawn from the U.S. Treasury unless authorized by Congress and a regular accounting of all dollars spent must be made available to the public.

Article 1, Section 9, clause 8. No title of nobility shall be granted by the United States; and no person holding any office of profit or trust under them, shall, without the consent of the Congress, accept of any present, emolument, office, or title, of any kind whatever, from any king, prince, or foreign state.

No titles of nobility (i.e., king, prince, duchess, etc.) shall be granted by the U.S. government; nor can anyone in the service of our government be allowed to accept a title from a foreign power.

Prohibitions on the States

Article 1, Section 10, clause 1. No state shall enter into any treaty, alliance, or confederation;

grant letters of marque and reprisal;

coin money; emit bills of credit;

make anything but gold and silver coin a tender in payment of debts;

pass any bill of attainder;

ex post facto law,

or law impairing the obligation of contracts,

or grant any title of nobility.

Article 1, Section 10, clause 2. No state shall, without the consent of the Congress, lay any imposts or duties on imports or exports, except what may be absolutely necessary for executing its inspection laws; and the net produce of all duties and imposts, laid by any state on imports or exports shall be for the use of the treasury of the United States; and all such laws shall be subject to the revision and control of the Congress.

Article 1, Section 10, clause 3. No state shall, without the consent of Congress, lay any duty of tonnage, keep troops or ships of war in time of peace, enter into any agreement or compact with another state, or with a foreign power, or engage in war, unless actually invaded, or in such imminent danger as will not admit of delay.

No state can make a treaty with a foreign country;

grant private citizens the right to capture ships from other countries;

coin its own money;

use anything other than gold or silver as a standard of money;

pass a bill of attainder (laws declaring a specific person guilty of breaking the law);

pass an ex post facto law (law that would punish someone for doing something that was not illegal when it was done);

pass laws that excuse people from their legal obligations under contract law;

grant titles of nobility.

With the approval of Congress . . . no state may lay a tax on goods imported or exported. However, an inspection fee may be charged. Any import/export taxes approved by Congress must go into the United States Treasury.

No state may tax ships or keep troops or ships during peacetime, make treaties with other states or foreign countries, or go to war unless attacked and in such danger that delay would be harmful to the state.

WHAT CONGRESS CANNOT DO

1. What is the difference between an ex post facto law and a bill of attainder? _____
   _____
   _____

   Both sound so unfair that it makes one wonder why the framers of the Constitution
   would even bother mentioning. Why did they include this paragraph? _____
   _____
   _____
   _____

2. What is the main essential in a writ of habeas corpus? _____
   _____
   _____

3. What purpose did Article 1, Section 9, clause 1 serve? _____
   _____
   _____
   _____

4. Define letters of marque and tell why you think Congress was forbidden from granting them under the Constitution. _____
   _____
   _____
   _____

5. Why are titles of nobility outlawed by the Constitution? _____
   _____
   _____

6. How did the 16th Amendment to the Constitution modify Article 1, Section 9,
   clause 4? _____
   _____
   _____

Article II—Executive Department

Article 2 presents the powers and duties of the President who is the Chief Executive. He is the man most responsible for enforcing the laws made by Congress. As you go through Article 2, you will see reasons for the framers of the Constitution outlining the powers and rules of the presidency as they did. You will also see why some of the things they did did not work and had to be later changed by amending the Constitution.

Article 2, Section 1, clause 1. The *executive* power shall be vested in a *President* of the United States of America. He shall hold his office during the term of four years, and, together with the Vice-President, chosen for the same term, be elected as follows:

Article 2, Section 1, clause 2. Each state shall appoint, in such manner as the legislature thereof may direct, a number of *electors,* equal to the whole number of senators and representatives to which the state may be entitled in the Congress; but no senator or representative, or person holding an office of trust or profit under the United States, shall be appointed an elector.

President Defined

The executive power (the power to execute the laws) shall be held by the President of the United States. The President shall serve a four-year term of office. There will also be a Vice-President elected at the same time for the same term of office.

Electors Elect the President

The President is elected by *electors.* These electors in each state are chosen in the manner prescribed by the state legislatures. Each state is entitled to a number of electors equal to its number of senators and representatives in Congress. But representatives and senators are not allowed to be electors themselves. It is these electors who actually choose the President. *Many people could not read and write at the time the Constitution was written. They were also poorly informed on matters of the day because there was no media to speak of. Thus the framers of the Constitution felt that the election of the President could best be placed in the hands of a few who were educated and did know the candidates and what each represented. It didn't take long, however, for the various state legislatures to allow the people to choose their electors and eventually it became as it is today. The electors collectively are called the Electoral College, and they still actually elect the President. But the people in each state vote on who will become their electors, depending on who they want to be their President. Thus in reality it is the people who are electing the President.*

Article 2, Section 1, clause 3. The electors shall meet in their respective states, and vote by ballot for two persons, of whom one at least shall not be an inhabitant of the same state with themselves. And they shall make a list of all the persons voted for, and of the number of votes for each; which list they shall sign and certify, and transmit sealed to the seat of the government of the United States, directed to the president of the Senate. The president of the Senate shall, in the presence of the Senate and House of Representatives, open all the certificates, and the votes shall then be counted. The person having the greatest number of votes shall be the President, if such number be a majority of the whole number of electors appointed; and if there be more than one who have such majority, and have an equal number of votes, then the House of Representatives shall immediately choose by ballot one of them for President; and if no person have a majority, then from the five highest on the list the said house shall in like manner choose the President. But in choosing the President, the votes shall be taken by states, the representation from each state having one vote, a quorum for this purpose shall consist of a member or members from two-thirds of the states, and a majority of all the states shall be necessary to a choice. In every case, after the choice of the President, the person having the greatest number of votes of the electors shall be the Vice-President. But if there should remain two or more who have equal votes, the Senate shall choose from them by ballot the Vice-President.

Method of Election

This paragraph tells how the President was originally elected. Bear in mind that this method was changed by the 12th Amendment. The electors met in their states and voted for two men, one of which had to live in another state. A list was then compiled of all those receiving votes and the number of votes each received. The lists were opened before a joint session of Congress. The man having the greatest number of votes became President. If he failed to achieve a majority of all the electors cast, then the President was chosen from the five who had the most votes by the House of Representatives. If there was a tie, the House of Representatives also elected the President. In such elections, each state shall have one vote and two-thirds of the states must be present. After the choice for the President was made, the electors chose the Vice-President. He was the man who came in second in the election for the presidency. If there was a tie for Vice-President, the Senate would elect the Vice-President.

Article 2, Section 1, clause 4. The Congress may determine the time of choosing the electors, and the day on which they shall give their votes; which day shall be the same throughout the United States.

Article 2, Section 1, clause 5. No person except a natural-born citizen, or a citizen of the United States at the time of the adoption of this Constitution, shall be eligible to the office of President; neither shall any person be eligible to that office who shall not have attained to the age of thirty-five years, and been fourteen years a resident within the United States.

Article 2, Section 1, clause 6. In case of the removal of the President from office, or of his death, resignation, or inability to discharge the powers and duties of the said office, the same shall devolve on the Vice-President, and the Congress may by law provide for the case of removal, death, resignation or inability, both of the President and Vice-President, declaring what officer shall then act as President, and such officer shall act accordingly, until the disability be removed, or a President shall be elected.

Article 2, Section 1, clause 7. The President shall, at stated times, receive for his services, a compensation, which shall neither be increased nor diminished during the period for which he shall have been elected, and he shall not receive within that period any other emolument from the United States, or any of them.

When Electors Are Chosen

Congress shall determine the date when electors will be chosen. *That date has come to be known as the Tuesday after the first Monday in November in all years evenly divisible by four. The Electoral College then cast their votes on the Monday after the second Wednesday in December following the November elections.*

Qualifications for President

To become President of the United States, one must be a natural-born U.S. citizen, at least 35 years of age and have lived in the United States for 14 years.

Vacancy in the Presidency

In the event of a vacancy occurring in the presidency, the Vice-President would assume the duties of the President. Congress would then decide by law who would be next in line should the Vice-President also become unable to serve as President. *This line of succession to the presidency and the procedures involving the Vice-President assuming the duties of the President have been changed and more clearly defined by the 25th Amendment.*

Rules Affecting the President's Salary

The President shall receive a salary which cannot be raised nor lowered during his term of office. The President may not receive any other salary from the United States or from any state while he is in office.

The Oath of Office

Article 2, Section 1, clause 8. Before he enter on the execution of his office, he shall take the following oath or affirmation:—"I do solemnly swear (or affirm) that I will faithfully execute the office of President of the United States, and will to the best of my ability, preserve, protect and defend the Constitution of the United States."

Before becoming President, the man elected to the position must take the following oath of office: "I do solemnly swear (or affirm) that I will faithfully execute the office of President of the United States and will to the best of my ability preserve, protect and defend the Constitution of the United States." *This condition of office (accepting this oath) is usually administered by the Chief Justice of the Supreme Court at the President's inauguration, which usually occurs on January 20.*

Looking back at... Article II, Section 1

Below are the answers to a crossword puzzle containing some important words in Article 2, Section 1. Make up the clues that go with the answers.

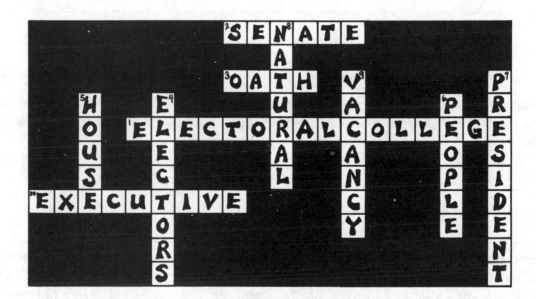

Clues:

1. _____ 6. _____

2. _____ 7. _____

3. _____ 8. _____

4. _____ 9. _____

5. _____ 10. _____

1. Why did the framers of the Constitution create the electoral system?

_____

_____

_____

_____

2. Under the original Constitution, what was wrong with the method used for choosing the President and Vice-President?

_____

_____

_____

How was the problem overcome with the 12th Amendment?

_____

_____

_____

_____

3. What purpose does the 7th clause serve in Article 2, Section 1? What problem can you see if the President's salary could be "adjusted" by Congress while he is in office?

_____

_____

_____

4. There has been much talk for many years about the pros and cons of having a woman become President. In 1984 Geraldine Ferraro ran as the vice-presidential candidate with Walter Mondale on the Democratic party ticket. They did not win but many considered Ms. Ferraro's running was a giant stride toward having a woman for our President. What are your own views about a woman becoming Chief Executive? Present both sides of the issue as best you can—then draw your own conclusion.

_____

_____

_____

_____

_____

_____

★ A MAN OF MANY HATS ★

It has often been said that the President of the United States has the "toughest job in the world." He must make decisions and take action every day on a wide variety of issues. The job itself involves successfully filling at least seven different roles in addition to those he performs as head of his own family. Briefly summarized below are the seven hats he wears.

Head of State: He is the living symbol of this nation, and he must provide an inspiring example for the American people.

Chief Executive: He is responsible for enforcing the laws of the United States as well as being in charge of bossing the thousands of government workers within the Executive Department.

Chief Foreign Policy Maker: With the help of his advisors, he establishes foreign policy and decides how America will react to certain foreign issues.

Commander in Chief: He is in charge of the Army, the Navy, the Air Force and the Marines.

Chief Legislator: Although Congress makes the laws, the President has a great deal of influence in deciding which legislation will be passed.

Chief of Party: He is also the leader of his party. Thus he must constantly be campaigning for others in his party who are seeking election.

Watchdog of the Economy: His role here is to do his best to fight inflation and to create a prosperous U.S. economy. He also prepares the nation's budget.

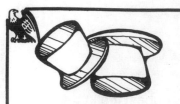

Match the action being taken by the President (by letter) with the role he is performing in each of the following. There may be some examples of his wearing more than one hat at the same time.

A. CHIEF EXECUTIVE
B. COMMANDER IN CHIEF
C. CHIEF OF PARTY
D. WATCHDOG OF THE ECONOMY

E. CHIEF FOREIGN POLICY MAKER
F. HEAD OF STATE
G. CHIEF LEGISLATOR

1. _____ Making a patriotic speech on Memorial Day
2. _____ Hosting a cabinet meeting to discuss foreign policy
3. _____ Signing a bill sent to him by Congress
4. _____ Sending in the National Guard to help flood victims in Florida
5. _____ Traveling to Iowa to make a speech at a benefit dinner for a party nominee to Congress
6. _____ Meeting with labor leaders to discuss a strike by auto workers
7. _____ Hosting a party in honor of a diplomat from The People's Republic
8. _____ Greeting visitors who come to the White House
9. _____ Hosting a brunch in the White House for the leaders of the Ways and Means Committee
10. _____ Awarding commissions to those who have recently graduated from West Point
11. _____ Choosing a member of his party to serve in the capacity of Secretary of Education
12. _____ Delivering his annual State of the Union message before the Congress
13. _____ Nominating someone to fill a vacancy created in a federal judgeship
14. _____ Officially receiving the Prime Minister of England
15. _____ Meeting with his cabinet on a regular basis
16. _____ Making a big pitch before the American people to help him fight a tax hike proposed by Congress
17. _____ Telling Congress he wants a mandatory seat belt law nationwide
18. _____ Releasing 9,000 government workers he feels are no longer necessary
19. _____ Meeting with Arab oil leaders to help establish a more stable price for oil
20. _____ Commuting to life imprisonment the death sentence of a terrorist who set off a bomb in a Denver airport terminal

ELECTING THE PRESIDENT

The men who wrote the Constitution planned for the best two candidates to become President and Vice-President. This theory was fine until political parties began to emerge. When this happened, the 12th Amendment became necessary. It was ratified in 1804, and since then each political party runs both a candidate for President and one for Vice-President. The framers of the Constitution did not feel that the people were qualified to vote for their President. Rather the President was elected by the Electoral College, which was made up of the electors from each state.

The number of electors each state was allowed was equal to the number of representatives it had in Congress (based on population) plus two (the number of U.S. senators in each state).

As the country grew and more states were added, more electors were included in the Electoral College. That number of electors was eventually frozen at 535. In 1961 the 23rd Amendment granted the citizens of Washington, D.C., the privilege of voting for President, too. That added three more electors (the minimum number a state can have) to the Electoral College, making the total 538. At the beginning of each decade, a census is taken and any major population shifts can result in some states getting additional electors, while others may lose some.

1. Look in an almanac or political directory to find the number of electors each state was entitled to in the last presidential election. Place those numbers within the boundaries of the states on the map on the following page.

2. How many electors did your state have in the last election? _____

3. Find out which candidate your state voted for in the last election. _____

4. Find out what determined the candidate the electors voted for in the Electoral College.

   _____

5. How many electors must a candidate have to win the presidency? _____

6. If you were running for President, in which states would you spend most of your

   time and money campaigning? _____

   _____

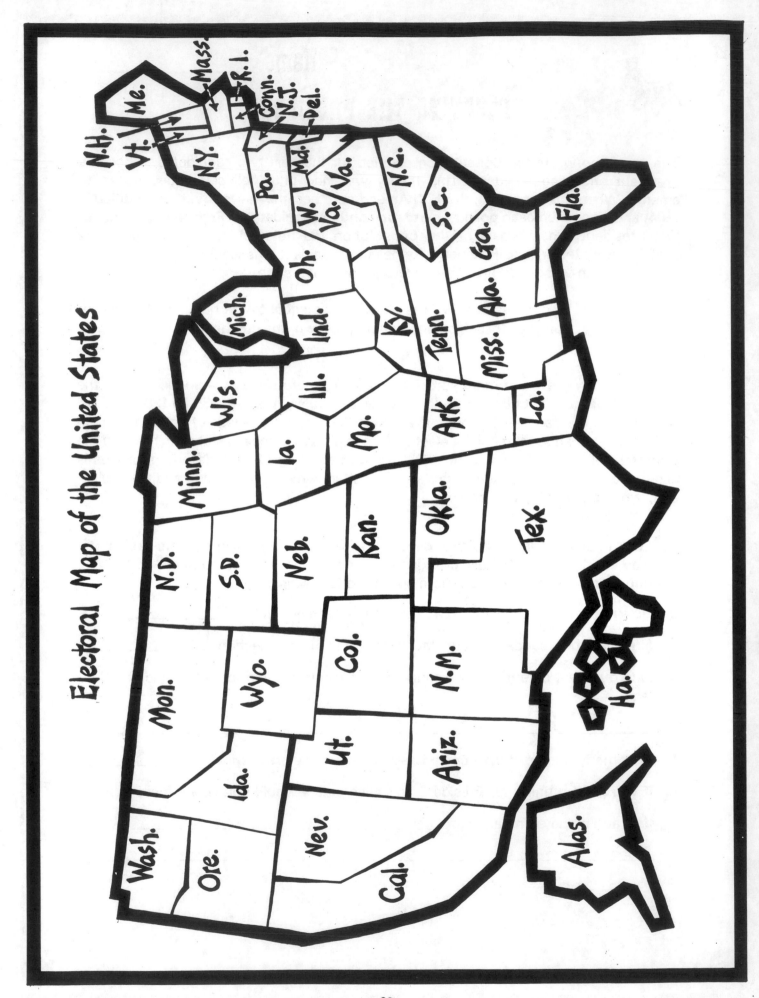

Electoral Map of the United States

ALL THE PRESIDENT'S MEN

The President of the United States has the most important job in the world. Without help from thousands of other people, he would never get his job done. Those who are directly responsible to him are called the members of his *cabinet.* Each of these cabinet members is in charge of a major area of concern to us. He in turn has literally hundreds of people either directly or indirectly responsible to him in gathering information and solving problems concerned with his specific concern. He is then directly responsible for keeping the President informed of the work within his department.

Your task is to research from another source the duties of these various cabinet posts and then to identify them with the statements on the next page. Then name the person who currently heads each of the departments.

1. ____Department of Health and Human Services

2. ____Department of the Treasury

3. ____Department of Justice—Attorney General

4. ____Department of Defense

5. ____Department of the Interior

6. ____Department of Energy

7. ____Department of State

8. ____Department of Agriculture

9. ____Department of Transportation

10. ____Department of Housing and Urban Affairs

11. ____Department of Labor

12. ____Department of Commerce

13. ____Department of Education

a._____ This man or woman is mainly responsible for promoting all phases of commerce, industry and business.

b._____ This person is responsible for managing our nation's finances. He is also responsible for the coining and printing of all money as well as enforcing all money laws, the Secret Service and the Coast Guard.

c._____ The cabinet head here is responsible for enforcing the laws of the United States in the federal courts. He is concerned with those matters in which the United States as a nation is involved in legal matters. He is the chief legal officer and conducts investigations into monopolies, antitrust laws, organized crime and the violation of conservation laws.

d._____ The leader here is charged with keeping a reasonable and proper balance of all the nation's resources, with preserving its scenic and historical landmarks, as well as being in charge of its National Parks and Forests, the Bureau of Indian Affairs and our nation's water supply.

e._____ This man is charged with handling all of our foreign affairs, including the participation of the United States in the United Nations. He is also responsible for issuing passports and maintaining our foreign embassies. He is perhaps the single most important of the cabinet members.

f._____ This "secretary" is charged with the general areas which his title suggests. They include the Public Health Service, the Social Security Administration, the Food and Drug Administration and the Office of Vocational Rehabilitation.

g._____ The cabinet leader here deals mainly with the complex transportation problems that face a "nation on the move" such as ours.

h._____ This man or woman is responsible for answering the problems of the growing needs of city dwellers and the many other implications of living in a large metropolitan area.

i._____ This "secretary" is responsible for defending our nation against all invaders. The main arm of his authority extends to our armed forces. He also advises the President on the billions of dollars spent annually on research to develop sophisticated armaments that will ensure our continued safety.

j._____ This cabinet leader is responsible for administering all phases of education from the kindergarten level through university post-graduate school.

k._____ The head of this department continually analyzes our present and future energy reserves. He also has been placed in the charge of implementing a national energy conservation program.

l._____ This department head is responsible for heading the nation's farm program. His job is concerned with getting a fair price for the American farmer and in stimulating sales of U.S. farm products to foreign countries.

m._____ He or she is in charge of the nation's labor supply. There are many complicated problems associated with reaching a balance between the available supplies of human labor and the demands for it. The head of this department constantly attempts to achieve that balance.

Military and Civil Powers of the President

Article 2, Section 2, clause 1. The President shall be *commander in chief* of the army and navy of the United States, and of the militia of the several states, when called into the actual service of the United States; he may require the opinion, in writing, of the principal officer in each of the executive departments, upon any subject relating to the duties of their respective offices, and he shall have power to grant reprieves and pardons for offenses against the United States, except in cases of impeachment.

The President shall be commander in chief of the armed forces. He also commands the National Guard when they are called into the service of the United States. He is also in command of all the executive departments and may require them to report to him in writing of the progress and actions going on within their departments. He also has the power to grant reprieves and pardons for those convicted of federal crimes with the exception of cases involving impeachments. *In this paragraph two of the President's main roles are assigned. The writers of the Constitution wanted him in charge of the armed forces because they preferred a civilian to a military person to control the nation's army and navy. He is also its chief executive; and the heads of departments who report to him that are cited in this paragraph have come to be known as his cabinet. They are his chief advisors.*

Article 2, Section 2, clause 2. He shall have power, by and with the advice and consent of the Senate, to make treaties, provided two-thirds of the senators present concur;

and he shall nominate, and by and with the advice and consent of the Senate, shall appoint ambassadors, other public ministers and consuls, judges of the Supreme Court, and all other officers of the United States, whose appointments are not herein otherwise provided for, and which shall be established by law;

but the Congress may by law vest the appointment of such inferior officers, as they think proper, in the President alone, in the courts of law, or in the heads of departments.

Article 2, Section 2, clause 3. The President shall have power to fill up all vacancies that may happen during the recess of the Senate, by granting commissions which shall expire at the end of their next session.

Treaties and Appointments

The President shall have the power to make agreements (treaties) with foreign nations as long as his agreements are approved by two-thirds of the senators present when the agreement is voted on. He also has the power to nominate ambassadors to foreign nations, Supreme Court justices and other high ranking government officials as long as his appointments are approved by a simple majority of the senators present. Congress may by law allow the President the power to appoint lesser ranking officials without approval from the Senate, or Congress may allow the courts or the heads of departments to appoint these officials. *This paragraph says a lot though it's not very long. It places in the hands of the President his role of chief foreign policy maker (power to make treaties). It also empowers him to choose his own staff of chief advisors (cabinet), the important federal judges, foreign ambassadors and other high ranking officials. The framers of the Constitution built flexibility into the establishment of the bureaucracy by providing methods for choosing many government workers. Thousands of these employees are chosen now through the Civil Service Commission.*

Temporary Appointments

The President has the power to fill vacancies as they occur while the Senate is in recess. These temporary appointments expire at the end of the next session of Congress.

Article 2, Section 3. He shall from time to time give to the Congress information of the state of the Union, and recommend to their consideration such measures as he shall judge necessary and expedient;

he may, on extraordinary occasions, convene both houses, or either of them, and in case of disagreement between them, with respect to the time of adjournment, he may adjourn them to such time as he shall think proper;

he shall receive ambassadors and other public ministers;

he shall take care that the laws be faithfully executed, and shall commission all the officers of the United States.

Article 2, Section 4. The President, Vice-President and all civil officers of the United States, shall be removed from office on impeachment for, and conviction of, treason, bribery, or other high crimes and misdemeanors.

Duties/Obligations of the President

The President shall address Congress from time to time on his assessment of the state of the nation. His annual message to them (and to us) at the beginning of each session of Congress is called the State of the Union message. He shall recommend to them the legislation he wants them to consider making law. He may also call Congress into special session when he feels it necessary to the best interests of the nation. He may decide when Congress shall adjourn if they are in disagreement. He shall serve as the official host to receive foreign ambassadors and ministers. Finally, he has the responsibility for seeing that all laws are enforced, and he commissions all officers of the United States. *This clause is another that is loaded with importance to the power of the presidency. His recommendations to Congress place him in the role of our chief legislator. In receiving the official heads of foreign nations, he wears the hat of our head of state, and he serves as our chief executive when he sees that all laws of this country are faithfully executed and enforced.*

Removal from Office

The President, Vice-President and other civil officers of the United States government can be removed from office if they are first impeached by the House of Representatives, then found guilty and convicted by the Senate. The grounds for such charges and convictions are only treason, bribery or other high crimes and misdemeanors. *Treason is defined as providing aid to the enemy. High crimes are those considered serious crimes, and misdemeanors are less important crimes.*

Looking back on... Article II, Sections 2-4

Below are some important facts to remember from Article 2. You provide the questions without looking at any of your notes or other assignment work papers.

1. to enforce the laws _____
   _____

2. the President of the United States _____
   _____

3. Chief Executive _____
   _____

4. Commander in Chief _____
   _____

5. four years _____

6. Vice-President _____
   _____

7. number of representatives plus number of senators in a state _____
   _____

8. January 20 _____

9. 35 years old, 14 years a resident of the United States, natural-born U.S. citizen ____
   _____

10. cabinet _____

11. ⅔ of the U.S. Senate _____

12. treason _____

13. the Electoral College _____

14. 13 _____

15. Chief Justice of the Supreme Court _____
    _____

16. simple majority of the Senate _____
    _____

17. 538 _____

ARTICLE III—JUDICIAL DEPARTMENT

The men who wrote our Constitution outlined and defined the powers and duties of our court system in Article 3. Although only the most powerful court—the Supreme Court—is clearly named, provision was made for lower courts to be created as needed by Congress and to empower Congress to also determine which cases are to be heard by the various courts within the framework of the judicial system. The main purpose of our courts is to decide how to settle issues when two parties are opposed to each other. The normal procedure is for a judge or jury to hear the arguments and evidence of both sides and then decide which is right, based on the law. Once that decision is made, the court then decides how the case is to be settled, whether it be ordering one party to pay money to the other, or in the case of criminal cases, deciding the penalty to be paid. Finally, our courts serve as the vehicle for interpreting our laws. This task is mainly done by the Supreme Court with the lower courts following their precedents.

The Court System

Article 3, Section 1. The judicial power of the United States, shall be vested in one Supreme Court, and in such inferior courts as the Congress may from time to time ordain and establish. The judges, both of the supreme and inferior courts, shall hold their offices during good behavior, and shall, at stated times, receive for their services, a compensation, which shall not be diminished during their continuance in office.

The power to make decisions in court cases shall be given to the Supreme Court and to lower courts established by Congress. The judges who oversee these courts shall hold office for life unless found guilty of misconduct. Their salaries cannot be lowered while they are in office. *In this paragraph Congress was given the power to establish lower courts as needed. Since that time Congress has indeed eliminated those courts no longer needed and created new ones whenever necessary. The Supreme Court is the most important court and rules over all other courts. Beneath it lie the 11 circuit courts of appeal; and beneath them are found the 90 district courts, which is where a case involving federal law begins. There are also other special courts created by Congress to deal with specific types of cases.*

Article 3, Section 2, clause 1. The judicial power shall extend to all cases, in law and equity, arising under this Constitution, the laws of the United States, and treaties made, or which shall be made under their authority;
—to all cases affecting ambassadors, other public ministers and consuls;
—to all cases of admiralty and maritime jurisdiction;
—to controversies to which the United States shall be a party;

—to controversies between two or more states;
between a state and citizens of another state;

—between citizens of different states;

—between citizens of the same state claiming lands under grants of different states; and between a state, or the citizens thereof, and foreign states, citizens or subjects.

The Power of Federal Courts

The power of the federal courts extends to all cases involving the Constitution, the laws of the United States and treaties made with foreign countries. In addition federal courts cover:
. . . all cases involving ambassadors of foreign countries
. . . cases involving ships
. . . cases in which the U.S. government is one of the parties involved
. . . cases where one of the states and citizens of another state are involved
. . . cases between citizens of different states
. . . cases involving disputes over grants of land
. . . cases where one of the states and a foreign country or its citizens are the parties involved
. . . cases where an American citizen and a foreign country or its citizens are the parties involved
The 11th Amendment removed the power of federal courts from hearing cases between a state and the citizens of another state. Also, while this paragraph gives federal courts the power to hear cases involving the Constitution, it doesn't clearly define what has come to be known as judicial review, i.e., the power to determine whether or not a law made by Congress falls within the framework of the Constitution. This power is one of the checks used by the judicial department over both the legislative and executive branches of our government.

Article 3, Section 2, clause 2. In all cases affecting ambassadors, other public ministers and consuls, and those in which a state shall be party, the Supreme Court shall have original jurisdiction. In all the other cases before mentioned, the Supreme Court shall have appellate jurisdiction, both as to law and fact, with such exceptions, and under such regulations as the Congress shall make.

Cases Heard by the Supreme Court

In cases involving foreign ambassadors or states, the Supreme Court has original jurisdiction. Original jurisdiction is defined as the right to hear a case for the first time and make a decision. In all other cases brought before the Supreme Court, it has appellate jurisdiction. Appellate jurisdiction is defined as reviewing a case that has already been heard in a lower court. Congress shall decide the types of cases that can be appealed. *Most federal cases begin in the U.S. District Courts. These courts have only original jurisdiction. Decisions reached by these courts can be appealed to the U.S. Court of Appeals. At this level the case is reviewed to see if there were any mistakes made in the handling of the case in the District Court that could have affected the decision of the jury. This appellate court does not hear any new evidence. Its task is to review what took place in the District Court. The Supreme Court has both original and appellate jurisdiction. Most of its case load comes from appeals brought from the Court of Appeals, but the Supreme Court decides which cases it will review. If a case is appealed to the Supreme Court from the Appellate and the Supreme Court refuses to hear the case, then the Appellate Court's decision is final. If the Supreme Court does choose to hear the case, then its decision becomes final. There are no appeals beyond the Supreme Court. The Supreme Court must be selective in the cases it hears because it could not possibly review all the cases that are appealed to it. The court chooses various kinds of cases involving points of law that need clarification and interpretation. Their decisions then serve as landmarks in lower courts who can refer to the decision of the Supreme Court in future similar cases.*

Article 3, Section 2, clause 3. The *trial* of all crimes, except in cases of impeachment, shall be by *jury*; and such trial shall be held in the state where the said crimes shall have been committed; but when not committed within any state, the trial shall be at such place or places as the Congress may by law have directed.

Article 3, Section 3, clause 1. Treason against the United States, shall consist only in levying war against them, or in adhering to their enemies, giving them aid and comfort. No person shall be convicted of treason unless on the testimony of two witnesses to the same overt act, or on confession in open court.

Article 3, Section 3, clause 2. The Congress shall have power to declare the punishment of treason, but no attainder of treason shall work corruption of blood or forfeiture except during the life of the person attainted.

Trial by Jury

Anyone accused of committing a crime has a right to a trial by jury, and that trial must be held in the state where the crime was committed. If the crime did not take place in any state, then Congress shall decide where the case will be heard.

Treason

Treason is defined in the Constitution as levying war against the United States or helping its enemies. No one can be convicted of treason unless at least two witnesses to the act testify against him in court or if the accused confesses to the deed in open court.

Punishment for Treason

Congress shall determine the punishment for treason, but the punishment must not extend to the guilty person's relatives. No corruption of blood means that the family members of the guilty must not suffer for his deeds, nor can they have their property taken away.

ORIGINAL VS. APPELLATE JURISDICTION

There are two kinds of jurisdiction which a court may have. They are *original* and *appellate*. Original jurisdiction is the power of a court to hear a case for the first time and pass judgment on that case. Decisions reached in courts with original jurisdiction are based on the judgment of twelve unbiased persons called a jury. A judge presides over the trial. After they have heard all the evidence, these twelve jurors leave the courtroom and go into deliberation, discussing all the evidence that has been presented by both sides. Then they vote. The voting must be unanimous for them to reach a decision. If all twelve are not in agreement, they must discuss the evidence again and vote until they do reach a unanimous decision. If they vote many times and spend many hours in deliberation without reaching a decision, they return to court and report that they are hopelessly deadlocked. This is called a *hung jury*, and it has the same effect as if no trial had even taken place. Judges and the court system dislike it very much when juries cannot reach a decision because of the time wasted. But there are situations when a jury simply cannot reach a unanimous decision.

Appellate jurisdiction is the power to review a case that has already been heard in a lower court. The decision of the Appellate Court may either uphold the lower court or it may reverse the lower court's decision. In the Appellate Court there is no jury. No new evidence is heard in the Appellate Court. The judge reviews the testimony and all other matters related to the case as it was heard in the District Court. On the basis of his findings, he can either uphold the ruling of the lower court or he can reverse the District Court's decision.

Using the information you were provided in Article 3 and the above, create a simple diagram showing the structure of our federal court system. Your drawing should portray the ranking and type of jurisdiction at each level.

Name _____

BECOMING A FEDERAL JUDGE

1. In this country where most of our public officials are elected by the people they serve, why do you think the men who wrote the Constitution provided for federal judges to be appointed by the President for terms of life?

   _____

   _____

   _____

   _____

   _____

   _____

2. What problems can you see that might occur as a result of judges being appointed for life?

   _____

   _____

   _____

   _____

   _____

   _____

   _____

3. How can they be solved?

   _____

   _____

   _____

4. What two steps are involved in obtaining a federal judgeship?

   a. _____

   b. _____

Name _____

PINPOINTING JURISDICTION

1. The Supreme Court is the single most powerful judicial force in the United States. It cannot be overruled. It is the final authority. Its decisions serve as a guiding light to the decisions reached in lower courts. It is composed of nine members who must be nominated by the President, approved by the U.S. Senate and serve for life. Their decisions become firm with a simple majority vote of 5-4. The members are referred to as justices, and the head of the court is called the Chief Justice. Find out the names, ages and years of service of each of the present court members.

Name	Age	Years on Court

2. Look in current news magazines and newspapers to find out about some of the more recent rulings handed down by the Supreme Court. Clip them and bring them to class. Post them on a special area of the bulletin board to share with others. As you and your classmates analyze the ruling in each case, determine the following:

    a.   the type of jurisdiction
    b.   the focus or point of law that brought the case before the Supreme Court
    c.   the "opinion" or reason cited for the court's eventual decision
    d.   the effect of the decision, i.e., who will be most affected and how

3. The Supreme Court has both original and appellate jurisdictions. While most of its case load is directed toward ruling on appeals from lower courts (appellate), there are occasions when the court hears a case for the first time. Decide the kind of jurisdiction the Supreme Court has in each of the following:

a. _____ The court rules that teaching is the kind of work where there is no clear relationship between age and ability to do the job; that knowledge and experience can actually increase a person's value in such jobs; that because of this the state of Mississippi cannot force Mary Ann Sullivan to retire from teaching just because she is 65 years old.

b. _____ Anthony Ray Wilson's lawyer is making a plea before the Supreme Court to overrule his client's prison sentence because he was convicted of a crime he committed while under the influence of a drug prescribed by his doctor.

c. _____ The ambassador to the United States from a small eastern Communist nation is arrested for breaking into a U.S. military missile site. When arrested he is found with copies of several top secret government documents.

d. _____ The court rules that certain literature being sent through the mail which the U.S. postmaster refuses to carry because of its subversive nature is not in violation of the sender's right to freedom of expression under the Constitution and orders him to stop immediately.

4. Where would you assign each of the following cases?

a. _____ A world renowned terrorist is linked to an explosive device that is found in a briefcase on a plane. Fortunately, the bomb was discovered before takeoff and removed without causing any damage or injury. The terrorist is arrested.

b. _____ The ambassador to the United States from a small Arab oil nation is arrested for a hit and run incident in which a young girl on a bicycle was seriously injured.

c. _____ Wilbur Conley was convicted of cheating the U.S. government by failing to report a large portion of his income to the IRS. Wilbur's lawyer claims that some of the evidence used against his client was gained illegally, and he wants to appeal the case.

d. _____ Former President Richard Nixon was accused of wrongdoing in the famous Watergate scandal. He resigned from office before he was ever brought to trial. If he had not resigned, where would his case have been heard?

CHECKS AND BALANCES

The men who wrote the Constitution wanted to be certain that no one person or group of persons could ever seize power and control the new American government. To ensure that this never happened, our United States government under the Constitution was divided into three parts: the *legislative,* the *executive* and the *judicial.* Each of these three branches has checks of power over the other two branches. These checks provide a system of balances in our government and that is why we call the system one of *checks and balances.*

These are the most important of the checks and balances:

The executive branch can check the legislative branch by vetoing laws.

The legislative branch can check the executive branch by passing laws over the veto by achieving a two-thirds majority vote in each house of Congress.

The judicial branch can check both the legislative and executive branches by declaring certain laws passed as being unconstitutional and thus invalid if they do not fall within the framework of the Constitution.

Obviously, this is not the whole system, but it is the main idea. Other checks and balances include these:

Executive over judicial—The President appoints all federal judges.

Legislative over executive—The legislative branch must approve all appointments made by the President. The Senate must approve treaties made by the President, and the legislative branch must investigate certain irregularities in the executive branch (like the uncover of Watergate).

Legislative over judicial—The legislative branch must approve of the President's choices for judicial appointments (judges).

Legislative over executive and judicial—The legislative branch has the power to impeach and remove from office all important federal officers.

Other Checks and Balances

There are other checks and balances in the American government besides those between the three branches of government. They include:

Senate and House of Representatives—The Senate and the House can check each other by rejecting bills passed by the other house. The House has the added check of the sole power to introduce revenue bills.

Checks on the People: A President is not elected directly by the people; only one-third of the Senate is elected at any one time; judges are not elected by the people.

Federalism: Another check is the theory of Federalism. This is a division of power between the national government and the state governments. In many ways this is a very natural division of power. Local affairs are handled by local governments; national affairs belong to the federal government. The Constitution lists certain specific powers that belong to the federal government. These are called *enumerated powers.* In addition Congress has the authority to pass laws that are "necessary and proper" in order to fulfill the purposes of the Constitution. Powers under this authority are called *implied powers.*

Since the Constitution does *not* list in detail the powers belonging to the states, there have been many conflicts over their respective powers. The Constitution does say that any "powers not delegated by the Constitution to the federal government are reserved to the states and to the people." These are called *reserve powers.*

THE SYSTEM AT WORK

Based upon what you just read about how the system of checks and balances works, indicate on the triangle below the powers each of the departments has over the other two. Some may be powers that check more than one branch. If so, indicate by placing the power on both lines.

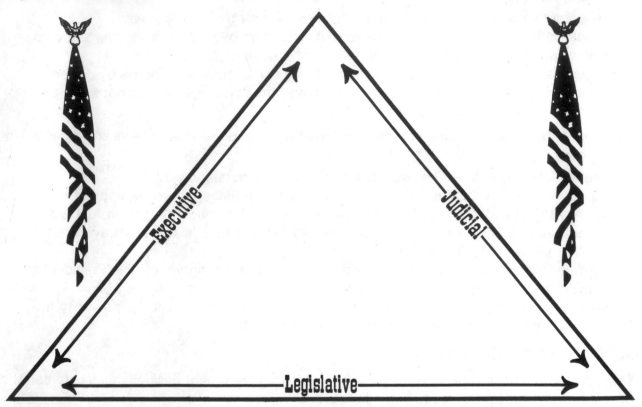

a. Can propose amendments to overrule judicial decisions
b. Can propose bills and call special sessions of the Congress
c. Can refuse to accept judicial appointments
d. Can declare laws unconstitutional
e. Can impeach and remove a President from office
f. Can grant pardons and reprieves
g. Can appoint all federal judges to office
h. Can override a presidential veto
i. Can refuse to ratify foreign treaties
j. Can refuse to approve of presidential appointments
k. Has the power of veto
l. Can declare executive acts unconstitutional
m. Can impeach and remove federal judges
n. As party leader, he can influence members of his party in Congress
o. Prepares the nation's annual budget

Name _____

THE CHECKS OF POWER

In each of the following situations, decide who has the power to "check" the wrong that is being committed.

1. The President is charged with being responsible for a break-in at the opposing party's headquarters. _____

2. Congress and the President approve a law that would prevent certain minorities from receiving tax exemptions which others are entitled to receive.

   _____

3. A young man convicted by the courts of being responsible for the deaths of thousands "during a wartime situation" has appealed his prison sentence to the Supreme Court. The court denied the motion to reverse the decision. There is a great deal of public support on his behalf.

   _____

4. A federal judge has been accused of "accepting large donations of stock certificates" from companies which have received some rather favorable rulings from him in the past. _____

5. Because one party has an overwhelming majority in both houses, the majority party has decided to pass "mass legislation" to help the party goals.

   _____

6. The President is tired of the hundreds of bills that have crossed his desk for action during the past two years. He decides in a moment of rage that he will "veto all bills . . . regardless of their nature . . . in the future."

   _____

7. The President makes a treaty with the Soviet Union in which the United States defense expenditures for the coming year are cut in half.

   _____

8. Three days before Congress is scheduled to adjourn, its members decide to deluge the President with huge numbers of "approved legislation" in the hope that he will hastily sign them into law without careful consideration.

   _____

9. The Supreme Court, which has been "leaning far too much toward the liberal" for the likes of the President, loses two of its members . . . one by death and the other through retirement. _____

10. There is an associate justice serving on the Supreme Court who is 88 years old. He is seldom able to attend sessions of the court because of illness; and when he is there, he seems to have lost that "razor-sharp" edge that earned him a spot on this high court so many years ago. In fact he is fast becoming senile!

    _____

Looking back at...
Original vs. Appellate

Name _____

Below are some definitions which will help you remember the most important elements in Article 3. Try to provide the answers without looking at your other notes and assignment papers.

1. _____ our most powerful court

2. _____ the U.S. court where most federal cases begin

3. _____ the federal court where appeals are heard

4. _____ the number of U.S. District Courts

5. _____ the number of Circuit Courts

6. _____ the kind of jurisdiction a court has when it hears a case for the first time

7. _____ the kind of jurisdiction a court has when it reviews the action of a lower court

8. _____ the power to determine whether or not a law made by Congress falls within the framework of the Constitution

9. _____ make the decisions reached in a district court

10. _____ the number of persons who serve on the U.S. Supreme Court

11. _____ defined as levying war against the United States or helping its enemies

12. _____ punishing the family members of one who has been convicted of a crime

13. _____ the number of witnesses required to testify in court against a person charged with treason

14. _____ the terms of office for federal judges

15. _____ the source of rulings in the circuit courts of appeal

16. _____ the vote needed to reach a decision in the Supreme Court

17. _____ the vote needed to reach a decision by the jury in U.S. District Courts

18. _____ federal judges are not elected to office. What are the two steps required to become a federal judge?

19. _____ the steps involved in removing a federal judge

20. _____ the title of the person who sits at the head of the Supreme Court

★ ARTICLE IV—THE RELATION OF THE STATES TO EACH OTHER ★

Once the separation of powers had been assigned and defined among the three branches of government, it became necessary to determine how the states were to interact and relate to each other. That was the purpose of Article 4.

Article 4, Section 1. Full faith and credit shall be given in each state to the public acts, records, and judicial proceedings of every other state. And the Congress may by general laws prescribe the manner in which such acts, records and proceedings shall be proved, and the effect thereof.

Full Faith and Credit

All states must respect the laws and court rulings of all other states. Congress shall make rules that will ensure that this happens.

Article 4, Section 2, clause 1. The citizens of the state shall be entitled to all privileges and immunities of citizens in the several states.

Citizen Rights in Other States

The citizens in each state have the same rights as the other citizens of that state.

Article 4, Section 2, clause 2. A person charged in any state with treason, felony, or other crime, who shall flee from justice, and be found in another state, shall on demand of the executive authority of the state from which he fled, be delivered up, to be removed to the state having jurisdiction of the crime.

Extradition

A person charged of committing a crime in one state cannot flee from justice by going to another state. Once captured, he shall be returned to the state in which the crime took place upon request of that state's governor. *This return of a prisoner to another state where a crime was committed is called extradition.*

Article 4, Section 2, clause 3. No person held to service or labor in one state, under the laws thereof, escaping into another, shall, in consequence of any law or regulation therein, be discharged from such service or labor, but shall be delivered up on claim of the party to whom such service or labor may be due.

Article 4, Section 3, clause 1. New states may be admitted by the Congress into this union;

but no new state shall be formed or erected within the jurisdiction of any other state;

nor any state be formed by the junction of two or more states, or parts of states, without the consent of the legislatures of the states concerned as well as of the Congress.

Article 4, Section 3, clause 2. The Congress shall have power to dispose of and make all needful rules and regulations respecting the territory or other property belonging to the United States;

and nothing in this Constitution shall be so construed as to prejudice any claims of the United States, or of any particular state.

Dealing with Runaway Slaves

Slaves and indentured servants could not become free men by simply escaping to a free state. Once caught, they were returned to their owners. *Slaves were defined as those forced to do the work of others. The 13th Amendment to the Constitution outlawed slavery. But this clause was placed in Article 4 to ensure that states honored the laws and rules of other states, even though there was a conflict of values over the issues associated with slavery.*

How New States Enter the Union

New states are admitted to the Union by Congress, but no state may be divided into other states without the approval of the states involved and Congress. In cases where two existing states want to unite to become a single state, both Congress and the states involved must agree to the Union. *Two states have been formed by dividing already existing states, but no states have been formed by uniting already existing states.*

Treatment of Territories

Congress shall have the power to sell or to give away land belonging to the United States. Congress shall also make laws to govern the territories. Nothing in the Constitution shall be interpreted to favor one state over another, or to favor a state in a disputed land claim. *The purpose of this paragraph was to give the Congress firm control over all U.S. territories. There was also some concern that some states might feel the Constitution would favor certain states. This paragraph was written to assure them this would not happen.*

Guarantees to All the States

Article 4, Section 4. The United States shall guarantee to every state in this union a *republican* form of government, and shall protect each of them against invasion; and on application of the legislature, or of the executive (when the legislature cannot be convened) against domestic violence.

The United States guarantees a republican form of government to every state in the Union. It shall also protect each state from invasion. Upon request by a state legislature or its chief executive, it will also help to stop riots within the state. *This paragraph guarantees a republican form of government to every state. This is a government where the people vote for their choices for those they wish to make the laws and enforce them.*

Name _____

FULL FAITH AND CREDIT CLAUSE

1. The full faith and credit clause (Article 4, Section 1) is one of the important statements made in the Constitution. Refer back to your reasons for the failure of the Articles of Confederation and explain why this paragraph was designed to overcome those problems.

   _____
   _____
   _____

2. The explanation in Section 3, clause 1, refers to two states being formed out of already existing states. Find out the names of these two states and the historical incidents that led to their being created by Congress.

   _____
   _____
   _____

3. Section 4 explains a republican form of government. Find out the differences between a true democracy and a republican form of government and tell why a true democracy would not be possible in the United States.

   _____
   _____
   _____
   _____

☆ ARTICLE V—AMENDING THE CONSTITUTION ☆

The men who wrote the Constitution designed it with a great deal of flexibility in mind, flexibility which you have already seen. But they knew that if the document were to withstand the test of time, they would have to provide for a reasonable way to change or add to it, as society itself would change over the generations and years time. Article 5 provides two such plans.

Procedures for Amending the Constitution

Article 5. The Congress, whenever two-thirds of both houses shall deem it necessary, shall propose amendments to this Constitution, or, on the application of the legislatures of two-thirds of the several states, shall call a convention for proposing amendments, which, in either case, shall be valid to all intents and purposes, as part of this Constitution, when ratified by the legislatures of three-fourths of the several states, or by conventions in three-fourths thereof, as the one or the other mode of ratification may be proposed by the Congress;

provided that no amendment which may be made prior to the year one thousand eight hundred and eight shall in any matter affect the first and fourth clauses in the ninth Section of the first Article;
and that no state, without its consent, shall be deprived of its equal suffrage in the Senate.

Amendments can be proposed in either of two ways. Two-thirds of both houses of Congress may propose a change, or an amendment may be proposed by having two-thirds of the state legislatures call for a special convention that will propose the amendment. Once an amendment is officially proposed, it must then be ratified to become a valid part of the Constitution. This ratification can occur in either of the following ways: the state legislatures in three-fourths of the states must vote for approval, or special conventions in three-fourths of the states can vote for approval. No amendment made prior to the year 1808 can affect the slave trade or provide for a different way of figuring taxes. No state without its consent can have its number of senators decreased. *There are two methods for proposing an amendment to the Constitution. Formally proposing an amendment is the first step. There are also two ways in which an amendment may be ratified, neither of which is without difficulty. Such is the way the framers of the Constitution wanted it to be. They wanted there to be enough flexibility to change the Constitution if change was necessary. But such change could not be accomplished without a great deal of effort and a genuine agreement among most of the people.*

Name _____

AMENDING THE CONSTITUTION

1. Find out the number of amendments that have been made to the original Constitution.

   _____

2. How many of those were proposed by Congress, and how many were proposed through special convention?

   _____

3. How many of the amendments were ratified by the state legislatures and how many were ratified by conventions held in the states?

   _____

4. Once a change to the Constitution has been officially proposed, find out how long it has until it must either be adopted as a part of the Constitution (by receiving proper ratification) or dropped for lack of achieving the required approval.

   _____

   _____

5. What is the number of states required to approve an amendment to the Constitution? _____

6. Research the battle over the Equal Rights Amendment of the 1970's and early 80's. What were the issues at stake? What was the eventual outcome?

   _____

   _____

   _____

   _____

   _____

   _____

   _____

   _____

There has been a lot of talk about amending the Constitution for this reason or that. Propose an amendment of your own and tell why you think it should become a part of the Constitution.

ARTICLE VI—GENERAL PROVISIONS

With the separation of powers defined, the relationship among the states established, and the rules set forth for amending the Constitution, it became a matter of just making these few final general statements. That is what Article 6 is about.

General Provisions

Article 6. All debts contracted and engagements entered into, before the adoption of this constitution, shall be as valid against the United States under this Constitution, as under the Confederation.

All debts and treaties entered into prior to the adoption of the Constitution shall be considered valid and will be honored by the United States.

This Constitution, and the laws of the United States which shall be made in pursuance thereof; and all treaties made, or which shall be made, under the authority of the United States, shall be the supreme law of the land; and the judges in every state shall be bound thereby, anything in the constitution or laws of any state to the contrary notwithstanding.

This Constitution shall be the supreme law of the land. All laws made by Congress and all treaties entered into by the United States shall be made in accordance with its rules and provisions, and all state judges must follow its guidelines. If they find laws in their states which contradict the Constitution, they must rule in favor of the Constitution.

The senators and representatives before mentioned, and the members of the several state legislatures, and all executive and judicial officers, both of the United States and of the several states, shall be bound by oath or affirmation, to support this Constitution; but no religious test shall ever be required as a qualification to any office or public trust under the United States.

All members of Congress, the various state legislatures plus all officers of the executive and judicial departments, both at the federal and state levels are required to affirm by oath their promise to uphold and support the Constitution. But no official or public employee can ever be subjected to a religious test as a condition of his or her employment.

GENERAL PROVISIONS

1. The men who wrote the Constitution felt it necessary to insert the first paragraph under the general provisions of Article 6. What message were they announcing to the rest of the world through this statement? Remember that we were a newly formed nation that had fought for and won its independence but had floundered under the Articles of Confederation.

    _____

    _____

    _____

2. Find out the amount of money the United States owed (the national debt) at the time of the Constitution.

    _____

    _____

3. How does that original debt compare with the national debt today? (Find out the current debt from a recent almanac.)

    _____

    _____

4. What happens if there is ever a conflict between a state law and a federal law that falls within the framework of the Constitution?

    _____

    _____

5. Why do you think the writers of the Constitution insisted that there be no religious test given as a condition of any public employee's getting a job?

    _____

    _____

6. How does the philosophy expressed in the second paragraph of Article 6 differ from the philosophy of the old Articles of Confederation? The answer to the question is one of the key reasons that the Articles of Confederation did not work.

    _____

    _____

With the framework well-established and all the specifics in place, the only task that remained before the fathers of the Constitution was to determine how the Constitution would be approved by the states it would serve. That is what this last paragraph in the original document is all about. There had been many battles through the long months of hammering out the Constitution, and the members of the Convention wanted to make certain their work was adopted, so they were very careful in the rules they set up for ratification.

Article 7. The ratification of the conventions of nine states, shall be sufficient for the establishment of this Constitution between the states so ratifying the same. Done in convention by the unanimous consent of the states present the seventeenth day of September in the year of our Lord one thousand seven hundred and eighty seven and of the independence of the United States of America the twelfth. In witness whereof we have hereunto subscribed our names.

Ratification

The ratification of the Constitution shall be considered sufficient whenever conventions in nine of the states have approved. The Constitution was officially signed on September 17, 1787, the twelfth year after our independence, by the unanimous consent of the twelve states present. In witness to this, these were the names of those who signed. *The writers called for conventions to be held in the states rather than allowing the state legislatures to decide whether or not their states would ratify the Constitution. They did this because they felt conventions called for the specific purpose of ratification would be more likely to approve.*

attest William Jacksth Secretary

Delaware
Geo: Read
Gunning Bedford jun
John Dickinson
Richard Bassett
Jaco: Broom

Maryland
James McHenry
Dan of St Thos. Jenifer
Danl Carroll

Virginia
John Blair—
James Madison Jr.

North Carolina
Wm Blount
Richd. Dobbs Spaight
Hu Williamson

South Carolina
J. Rutledge
Charles Cotesworth Pinckney
Charles Pinckney
Pierce Butler

Georgia
William Few
Abr Baldwin

G. Washington—Presidt.
and deputy from Virginia

New Hampshire
John Langdon
Nicholas Gilman

Massachusetts
Nathaniel Gorham
Rufus King

Connecticut
Wm Saml Johnson
Roger Sherman

New York
Alexander Hamilton

New Jersey
Wil Livingston
David Brearley
Wm Paterson
Jona: Dayton

Pennsylvania
B Franklin
Thomas Mifflin
Robt Morris
Geo. Clymer
Thos FitzSimons
Jared Ingersoll
James Wilson
Gouv Morris

Name _____

RATIFYING ARTICLE VII

1. What was the requirement established by the Constitutional Convention for ratify-
    ing the new Constitution?

    _____

    _____

    _____

    _____

2. How many states were represented by the men who signed the Constitution? ____

3. Which state was not represented? _____

4. Which state had the most number of signatures on the original Constitution?

    _____

5. How many signatures are there on the original document? _____

6. Which state was the first to ratify the Constitution? _____

7. How long did it take between the time the Convention ended and the time when the
    nine states necessary for ratification had approved the Constitution?

    _____

    _____

    _____

Looking back on... Articles IV, V, VI, VII

Show your knowledge of Articles 4—7 by referring back to your notes to fill in the blanks below.

1. _____ transferring an accused criminal back to the state where a crime was committed

2. _____ the number of states needed to ratify the Constitution

3. _____ the article where the full faith and credit clause is found

4. _____ the source of power to admit new states into the Union

5. _____ the two states created when states already existing were divided

6. _____ the source of power to govern all U.S. territories

7. _____ the number of signatures on the original Constitution

8. _____ the date when the Constitution was signed

9. _____ the number of states needed to ratify an amendment to the Constitution

10. _____ the number of amendments to the Constitution

11. _____ the two steps necessary in amending the Constitution

12. _____ the national debt at the time the Constitution was written

13. _____ the state not represented when the Constitution was signed

14. _____ the two methods of proposing a constitutional amendment

15. _____ the two methods of ratifying a constitutional amendment

16. _____ the authority for deciding the method used in ratifying an amendment

17. _____ the Supreme Law of the Land

18. _____ the year the Constitution became effective

19. _____ It defines a political society in which the people elect their leaders who make the laws and enforce them.

20. _____ If a state is having problems with domestic violence (riots), this authority can ask for federal assistance to restore peace.

94

BILL OF RIGHTS

The men who wrote the original Constitution did not think it was necessary to list the individual rights of the people. They assumed that because the various state constitutions contained lists of individual rights, then it should not be necessary to place them in the U.S. Constitution. When copies of the new Constitution were dispatched to the states and the people for a "first look," they found out differently.

There was an overwhelming urge and insistence among the people that an assurance of the individual rights of man should be spelled out very clearly in the Constitution. Such was the condition under which several of the state conventions ratified the Constitution. They would ratify the document only if a bill of rights would be added. Congress was quick to comply.

The Constitution went into effect in 1789. In that same year it reviewed more than twenty amendments suggested by the ratifying convention. Congress pared the list down to twelve, which were submitted to the states to be ratified. Ten of them were approved and became part of the Constitution by 1791.

Because they followed so soon after the original document, they are looked at historically as almost being a part of the original document. But they clearly point to one of the first major uses of the Constitution as the framework of the American nation—namely the process involved in changing it (amending) to suit the needs of the people. These first ten amendments also point to the power of the people themselves to make certain that their own liberties were not overlooked.

The new Constitution had clearly defined the power of the federal government, and it had established the supremacy of the federal government over any and all state governments. The people wanted their rights protected, too. They got their wish in the form of the first ten amendments, known as the Bill of Rights.

Amendment 1

Congress shall make no law respecting an establishment of religion, or prohibiting the free exercise thereof;

or abridging the freedom of speech, or of the press;

or the right of the people peaceably to assemble, and to petition the government for a *redress of grievances.*

Freedom of Religion/ Political Freedoms

Congress can make no law that establishes an official religion, nor can it pass laws that prohibit people from following any religion they choose, as long as the practices of the religion do not violate any of our other laws;

nor can Congress pass laws that prohibit people from speaking and writing their thoughts;

nor can Congress pass laws that will prevent people from gathering together peacefully to discuss their government and appeal to it to correct any wrong they feel may have been done.

There are actually five freedoms very precious to the people pointed out in this 1st Amendment. They are freedom of religion, speech, press, assembly and petition. A good number of issues over these personal freedoms have ended up in court battles. They were intended to provide the people they serve with the freedoms necessary for self-expression; but they are not without limitations and restrictions. The courts must protect people from pursuing their own self-interests to the point of bringing harm to other people, or in some way violating their own personal rights. The letter of the law is unclear in some situations, and it takes a court to decide whether or not personal rights have been violated.

Amendment 2

A well regulated militia being necessary to the security of a free state, the right of the people to keep and bear arms shall not be infringed.

Amendment 3

No soldier shall, in time of peace be *quartered* in any house, without the consent of the owner, nor in time of war, but in a manner to be prescribed by law.

Amendment 4

The right of the people to be secure in their persons, houses, papers, and effects, against unreasonable searches and seizures, shall not be violated, and no warrants shall issue, but upon probable cause, supported by oath or affirmation, and particularly describing the place to be searched, and the persons or things to be seized.

The Right to Bear Arms

Because it is necessary to maintain a militia of men ready to defend the country, Congress does not have the right to keep people from owning and carrying arms (guns). *This issue has been a real hotbed in the past few years with terrorist attacks against private citizens becoming all too commonplace. On the other hand, the many assassination attempts on politically important people have caused Congress and the courts some doubts about our current gun laws.*

Quartering Soldiers

No soldier during peacetime can be forced into the homes of private citizens. And during war soldiers can be placed in private homes only in a manner as prescribed by Congress.

Search and Seizure

Unless a proper search warrant has been authorized, a person has a right to protect his own person, his home, his papers and his personal effects. A search warrant can only be issued through a court of law if proper explanation of why the search needs to be made has been provided. That explanation must include the place to be searched, the reason for the search and exactly who or what is expected to be found. *The people insisted on this protection for themselves and their property to prevent the police and the military from the unnecessary hassle and invasion of their property which many had experienced when the colonies were under the rule of England. They wanted no part of this in their new Constitution. If a search warrant is issued, the judge must be presented with solid evidence that there is good cause for issuing one.*

Amendment 5

No person shall be held to answer for a capital, or otherwise infamous crime, unless on a *presentment* or *indictment* of a *grand jury,* except in cases arising in the land or naval forces, or in the militia, when in actual service in time of war or public danger;

nor shall any person be subject for the same offense to be twice put in jeopardy of life or limb;

nor shall be compelled in any criminal case to be a witness against himself,

nor be deprived of life, liberty, or property, without *due process* of law;

Rights of the Accused in Court

No person shall be tried for a serious criminal act unless he has first been presented an indictment by a grand jury, except in cases involving members of the military during times of war or public danger.

An indictment is a formal charge that accuses a person of having committed a crime. That indictment is issued by a grand jury which examines the evidence against the accused to determine whether or not there will even be a trial. The grand jury is composed of 12-23 persons. If a simple majority of its members agree that there is enough evidence against the accused, a true bill is issued and the guilt or innocence of that accused person will be determined in a court of law by a petit jury, where both sides are heard.

Nor shall any person be subjected to double jeopardy.

The double jeopardy clause refers to the fact that a man cannot be tried a second time for a crime if he was found not guilty during an earlier trial.

Nor shall anyone be forced to say anything in court that could lead to his conviction;

nor can anyone be deprived of life, liberty or property without due process of law.

Due process of law is the sum total of the letter of the law as viewed by the courts. This statement is further assurance that the accused will be given a fair trial and none of his personal effects will be taken unfairly from him.

nor shall private property be taken for public use, without just compensation.

Nor can private property be taken for public use without the government paying a fair price for it.

The government does indeed have the right to take private land for public use. That right is called eminent domain. But if the courts do rule in favor of public use, then the government must pay the landowner a fair price for it.

Amendment 6

In all criminal prosecutions, the accused shall enjoy the right to a speedy and public trial, by an impartial jury of the state and district wherein the crime shall have been committed, which district shall have been previously ascertained by law, and to be informed of the nature and cause of the accusation;

to be confronted with the witnesses against him;

to have *compulsory process* for obtaining witnesses in his favor, and to have the assistance of *counsel* for his defense.

Additional Rights in Court

Anyone accused of committing a crime has a right to a speedy and public trial. The guilt or innocence of the accused shall be determined by an impartial jury made up of citizens that live in the state and district where the crime was committed. The accused must be given proper notification of the charge for which he or she is being tried.

The accused has the right to be present in court and to see face to face those who are witnesses against him.

The accused also has the right to call witnesses to court to testify in his behalf. Even if they do not wish to volunteer to appear in court, the accused has the right to force their compulsory attendance and testimony through a court order called a subpoena. The accused also has a right to be properly defended during his trial. If he cannot afford an attorney, the court will appoint one to serve in his behalf.

Amendment 7

In suits at *common law,* where the value in controversy shall exceed twenty dollars, the right of trial by jury shall be preserved, and no fact tried by a jury, shall be otherwise reexamined by any court of the United States than according to the rules of the common law.

Jury Trials

When there is a dispute over property where the value exceeds twenty dollars, either party can insist that a jury decide the issue. If the case is appealed to a higher court, that court must render a decision based upon the facts presented in that specific case. *Both parties may also agree to present their case before a judge and allow the judge to make the decision. This cuts down on the cost and helps to avoid the backlog of cases courts sometimes have.*

Amendment 8

Excessive *bail* shall not be required, nor excessive fines imposed, nor cruel and unusual punishments inflicted.

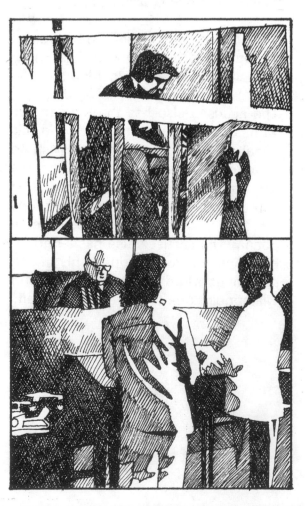

Excessive Bail and Punishment

Excessive *bail* shall not be allowed. Bail is the amount of money required by the court of the accused to ensure that he will show up for his trial if he is allowed to go free between the time of his capture and his trial. The punishments assessed by courts against those found guilty of committing crimes cannot be excessive nor can they be cruel or unusual. *The amount of bail allowing a person accused of committing a crime to go free until his trial is determined by a judge. Another guideline of this amendment insists that courts make the punishment suit the crime that has been committed. Excessive punishments are outlawed and the ''cruel and unusual'' rather barbaric punishments of early New England were also ruled out.*

Amendment 9

The enumeration in the Constitution of certain rights, shall not be construed to deny or disparage others retained by the people.

Amendment 10

The powers not delegated to the United States by the Constitution, nor prohibited by it to the states, are reserved to the states respectively, or to the people.

Other Rights

The listing of the specific personal rights of the people found in the Constitution does not mean that people do not have other rights. Those other rights may also be just as important as those listed. *Those who wrote the bill of rights soon realized that they could not list every single right afforded to individuals. So they put in the 9th Amendment to cover all those not listed. Some are quite obvious; some are not so obvious and have led to challenge in court.*

Rights of the States and the People

Those powers not specifically set aside for the federal government nor denied the states and the people are reserved for the states and the people. *Here again is another statement assuring those who would later interpret the Constitution that both the states and the people have rights in addition to those that appear in the Constitution.*

BILL OF RIGHTS

1st Amendment: The Five Freedoms

1. List the five freedoms in the 1st Amendment.

   a.

   b.

   c.

   d.

   e.

2. Our Constitution says a man may say or write anything he wants. There are, however, some limitations placed on this precious freedom. Can you think of any situations where someone would be restricted from expressing this freedom completely?

   _____

   _____

3. What are the possible consequences people risk when they refuse to respect the limits placed on freedom of speech and freedom of the press?

   _____

   _____

4. Can you think of any restrictions that might be placed upon a man's freedom to worship in whatever manner he so chooses?

   _____

5. What is the difference between the right to assemble and the right to petition?

   _____

   _____

2nd Amendment: Right of Protection

1. The 2nd Amendment established the right of a state to have a militia. What did it say about the right of private individuals owning weapons?

   _____

   _____

2. Have there since been any restrictions placed on man's constitutional right "to bear arms"? If so, what are they?

   _____

   _____

3rd Amendment: Quartering of Soldiers

During peacetime, no soldier shall be quartered in a house without the consent of the owner. Where do you think this idea came from?

_____

_____

_____

4th Amendment: Search and Seizure

1. Under the 4th Amendment, what items are protected from unwarranted searches?

_____

_____

_____

2. What information must be contained in an authorized search warrant?

_____

_____

_____

5th Amendment: Fair Trial in Open Court

1. What is the difference between a capital crime and an infamous crime?

_____

_____

2. No person can be punished for a capital crime or for an infamous crime without first having been indicted by a grand jury. What is an indictment?

_____

_____

3. What is the nature of the job of the grand jury?

_____

_____

4. How many persons are there on a grand jury?

_____

5. What is the difference between a ''true bill'' and a ''no true bill''?

_____

_____

6. What does the 5th Amendment mean when it talks about no one being placed in "double jeopardy"?

_____

_____

_____

7. You have heard the familiar phrase of a criminal in court who says: "I plead the 5th." What specific quote from the 5th Amendment is the defendant referring to when he says these words?

_____

_____

8. "No person may have his life, his liberty, or his property taken from him without 'due process of law.' " What does the phrase *due process of law* mean?

_____

_____

6th Amendment: The Rights of a Person in Court

1. In all cases of criminal prosecution, the accused shall have the right to a speedy trial. What does the Constitution say about the location of that trial?

_____

_____

2. The accused has the right to be judged by a jury of 12 unbiased persons and must be completely informed of all existing rights. One of those is to confront face to face those who testify against him. Why do you think the accused has this right?

_____

_____

_____

3. What do we call the court order which forces witnesses for the accused to appear and testify in court whether they want to or not?

_____

7th Amendment: Jury Trials

1. What is the minimum dollar amount over which a common lawsuit can be filed?

_____

2. The decision of the jury shall be final except under either of these two circumstances:
   a.
   b.

8th Amendment: Excessive Bail and Punishment

1. What is bail?

   _____

   _____

2. The 8th Amendment calls for bail to be appropriate for the crime committed. Neither can the fine imposed by the court be excessive for the crime committed. Nor can the courts call for cruel or unusual punishments for crimes committed. Trace the history of early colonial America and find some examples of "cruel and unusual punishment" which the men who wrote the Constitution must have had in mind when they wrote this paragraph?

   _____

   _____

3. The Supreme Court has the final word in deciding what is "cruel and excessive" punishment. On June 29, 1972, the Supreme Court ruled that capital punishment was unconstitutional on the grounds that it was being administered unfairly—that this manner in which it was being administered was in and of itself "cruel" and "excessive"—thus violating the 8th Amendment. Since that time the Supreme Court has reversed that decision; and as long as the punishment is administered fairly to all, it is no longer "cruel and excessive." This has paved the way for several executions in the United States. What is your own opinion?

   _____

   _____

9th Amendment: Other Rights

1. The 9th Amendment says that the Constitution has given us all certain rights. It cannot, however, list all of those rights. Just because a right is not listed in the Constitution does not mean that it does not exist. Give an example of one of those rights you have.

   _____

   _____

2. How is the 9th Amendment like Article 1, Section 8, last paragraph?

   _____

   _____

10th Amendment: Rights of the States and the People

What happens to all those powers that are not specifically given to the federal government?

_____

_____

OUR LIVING BILL OF RIGHTS

Decide which of the first ten amendments applies in each case below and explain the point of law that is the issue.

1. Angela Harrison and some of her friends are planning a rally in front of city hall to protect the new budget prepared by the President and Congress. Their main concern is that there is a large increase in defense spending to cover a new nuclear missile defense system. Angela has a reputation as being somewhat of a radical, and trouble usually follows wherever she goes. But even though armed police will be present, Mary has registered properly with the authorities, and they won't stand in her way even though they don't like it.

   _____

   _____

   _____

2. Anthony Morgan has a long history of dealing in drugs. In fact he's spent much of his adult life in and out of jail and prison. Anthony was watched by police for several weeks as they prepared to close in on him one more time. On September 23 authorities approached him at his home and presented him with a search warrant allowing them to search his home for drugs. Strange as it may seem, they didn't find any—not even so much as a marijuana cigarette. But what they did find in Morgan's basement made them equally interested: fourteen new television sets with the serial numbers scratched out and ten brand-new VCR's.

   _____

   _____

   _____

3. Randy Winegard just picked all six winning numbers in the Lotto and as a result will receive $250,000 each year for the next twenty years. Randy never did care much for his job, and so bright and early Monday morning he went into his office and quit his job on the spot, saying he planned to . . ."have some fun for a change."

   _____

   _____

   _____

4. Three young ruffians recently hid behind the bushes looking for someone to come by with something worth stealing. Mrs. McFeeters just happened to be in the wrong place at the wrong time and became their chosen victim. They planned to simply snatch her purse and run. But Mrs. McFeeters was far from the defenseless little old lady they'd bargained for. She carried a whistle around her neck and a can of mace in the purse they were trying to steal and she used both of these. She also bit one of the thugs on the arm and kicked another in the battle for her purse. In retaliation one of them knocked her down, and she cut her head requiring four stitches. But she got a good description of her assailants, and they were arrested less than an hour later. As they were thrown into a jail cell, they overheard one of the officers say, "We're gonna make sure the judge throws the book at these guys! What kind of low life would pick on a poor defenseless little old lady?"

_____

_____

_____

5. The meat packers union in Hamburger, Minnesota, has been on strike for the last four months over a salary/benefits dispute. The issue recently heated up when the owner of the packing company hired outside help to resume his business of packing meat. When these workers crossed the picket line, they were attacked by union members. There has been violence every day since. The National Guard has been called in to put down the violence and restore the peace. The leader of this unit has announced to the mayor of Hamburger that since it's wintertime and it's cold, and since his soldiers have no other place to stay, the mayor must find places for them to stay in the homes of Hamburger residents.

_____

_____

_____

6. Arthur Fairchild has been accused of breaking into a top secret military installation and tampering with the records contained therein. Authorities have a good case against Fairchild, and they have an excellent chance of getting a conviction. The only piece to the puzzle that doesn't fit is Fairchild's claim that on the night of the break-in, he was with "some friends" at a party sniffing cocaine. Because this is against the law, none of Fairchild's friends want to come forward and testify on his behalf.

_____

_____

_____

7. Mary Livingston owns a cabin on forty acres of wooded timberland near an absolutely beautiful lake in the foothills of North Carolina. The land and the cabin have been in her family for three generations; and Mary, who is a teacher, looks forward to every summer which she spends there. The federal government has been quietly buying up the land in the area to create a national park. They've offered Mary a price for her land, but she refused to sell. They came back with an even better offer, but she remains firm. "This is my land and it's not for sale at any price!"

    _____

    _____

    _____

8. Julie Moon recently got a good job as a legal secretary. Being a "small town girl," the big city scares Julie more than a little. To get to work from her apartment, she has to drive through a rough neighborhood where the crime rate is very high. But Julie carries some comfort with her in the form of a small handgun which her father gave her when she left for the city. Julie keeps the loaded weapon in her purse and says she'll "not hesitate to use it if trouble comes my way."

    _____

    _____

    _____

9. The Winfields and the McGrieves have been at odds ever since Hank McGrieve bought the property next to Thomas Winfield six months ago. The reason is that McGrieve had his new property resurveyed, and he found that a stately row of oak trees that separate the two properties actually stand on his land. He knows the value of oak and wants to cut down the trees and sell the wood. Winfield claims that the trees were planted by his "great-grandaddy over 100 years ago" as a nice division between the two properties, and he wants the trees to remain standing. Winfield has filed a lawsuit against McGrieve and wants a jury to decide the issue. Both properties lie within the boundary lines of a national forest.

    _____

    _____

    _____

10. Which of the amendments contained in the Bill of Rights have you not used? _____

    _____

Amendment 11

The judicial power of the United States shall not be construed to extend to any suit in law or equity, commenced or prosecuted against one of the United States by citizens of another state, or by citizens or subjects of any foreign state.

Cases Against the States

Private citizens of different states or of foreign countries cannot sue a state in federal court. *Many people felt that allowing such cases to be heard in federal courts as provided in the original Constitution under Article 3 gave the central government too much power.*

PRELUDE TO AMENDMENT 12

The men who wrote the original Constitution created a method for electing the President and Vice-President which they felt would get the nation the very best two men for these important jobs. The idea was very simple: the candidate who won the most electoral votes would become President; the candidate with the second greatest number of electors would be Vice-President. This plan worked out okay until the fourth election when political parties began to emerge. In the election of 1796, John Adams, who was a Federalist, was elected President and Thomas Jefferson, a Republican was elected Vice-President. These two men who were supposed to be working together were from entirely different political backgrounds and had conflicting political views.

But the election of 1800 was even worse. The Federalists supported John Adams and Charles Pinkney, and the Republicans supported Thomas Jefferson and Aaron Burr. The election for President was supposed to be between Jefferson and Adams, while the vice-presidency was to be contested between Burr and Pinckney. But both Jefferson and Burr ended up with the same number of 71 electoral votes with Adams getting 65 and Pinckney 64. Since no candidate had a majority, the Constitution provided for the election to be decided in the House of Representatives. Then each state would get one vote.

The Federalist party was not as strong as the Republican party and knew they could not win, but they could prevent someone else from winning, too. And prevent they did! They voted 35 times! Each vote ended in a tie. On the 36th ballot they gave in and abstained from voting to allow Jefferson to win the election. But such tactics made it quite clear that a new method for electing the President was sorely needed. Such was the work of the 12th Amendment.

Amendment 12

The electors shall meet in their respective states and vote by ballot for President and Vice-President, one of whom, at least, shall not be an inhabitant of the same state with themselves; they shall name in their ballots the person voted for as President, and in distinct ballots the person voted for as Vice-President, and they shall make distinct lists of all persons voted for as President, and of all persons voted for as Vice-President, and of the number of votes for each, which list they shall sign and certify, and transmit sealed to the seat of the government of the United States, directed to the president of the Senate;

The president of the Senate shall, in the presence of the Senate and House of Representatives, open all the certificates and the votes shall then be counted;

The person having the greatest number of votes for President, shall be the President, if such number be a majority of the whole number of electors appointed; and if no person have such majority, then from the persons having the highest numbers not exceeding three on the list of those voted for as President, the House of Representatives shall choose immediately, by ballot, the President. But in choosing the President, the votes shall be taken by states, the representation from each state having one vote; a quorum for this purpose shall consist of a member or members from two-thirds of the states, and a majority of all the states shall be necessary to a choice.

Electing the President

The electors would meet in their respective states where they separate ballots for the President and the Vice-President. At least one of the candidates they vote for must live in another state. The electors then make a list of all those who received votes for President and another list of those who won votes for Vice-President. They tally up the totals and send both lists to the president of the U.S. Senate.

In the presence of both houses of Congress, the president of the Senate opens the votes from each state and tallies the votes.

The person with the most votes becomes President if he has more than a single majority of all electors. If no one has a majority, then the House of Representatives shall elect the President. It chooses from a list of no more than three candidates. Each state has only one vote and there must be at least two-thirds of the states represented when this election takes place. The candidate who has the greatest number of votes shall become President.

And if the House of Representatives shall not choose a President whenever the right of choice shall devolve upon them, before the fourth day of March next following, then the Vice-President shall act as President, as in the case of the death or other constitutional disability of the President.

The person having the greatest number of votes as Vice-President, shall be the Vice-President, if such number be a majority of the whole number of electors appointed, and if no person have a majority, then from the two highest numbers on the list, the Senate shall choose the Vice-President; a quorum for the purpose shall consist of two-thirds of the whole number of senators, and a majority of the whole number shall be necessary to a choice.

But no person constitutionally ineligible to the office of the President shall be eligible to that of Vice-President of the United States.

If the House of Representatives should fail to choose a President by March 4 (the date when the newly elected President is supposed to assume his office), then the Vice-President shall act as President. *This part of the amendment was later changed by the 20th Amendment.*

The candidate with the greatest number of electoral votes for Vice-President shall become the Vice-President. But if that candidate does not have a simple majority of all electors, then the Vice-President shall be chosen by the U.S. Senate. The Senate chooses from a list of the two who had the greatest number of electors. Two-thirds of the senators must be present when the vote is taken and the candidate who wins must have a simple majority vote of all the U.S. senators.

No person constitutionally ineligible to become President shall be eligible to become Vice-President either.

THE BIRTH OF ALL PARTIES

Article 2 clearly spells out that the President and the Vice-President shall be elected by the Electoral College made up of electors from each state. The number of electors a state has is dependent upon its population, as each state has as many electors as it has senators plus representatives. When people vote in a presidential election, they are actually casting their votes for the electors pledged to the candidate of their choice.

Under the original Constitution there was no distinction between the candidates who ran for President and those who ran for Vice-President. Each elector voted for two people from the list of candidates. The person with the highest total became President and the runner-up became the Vice-President.

When George Washington was elected President, he was elected unanimously. There were sixty-nine electors and they all voted for him. John Adams had the second highest total of the men on the list, so he became Vice-President. There weren't any political campaigns because there weren't any political parties.

Political parties emerge when a significant number of people all have the same philosophy and a number of common goals. Such was the case in America. Alexander Hamilton and Thomas Jefferson were both great statesmen chosen by Washington to serve in his cabinet. But they had conflicting political views. Hamilton believed in a strong central government and thus wanted a loose interpretation of the Constitution to allow for the Congress and the President and the courts to have latitude to make the decisions that needed to be made. Jefferson believed in the power of the state and local authorities to make their own decisions. His position was thus one of restricting the power of the federal government to a strict interpretation of the Constitution. Jefferson's followers became known as the Democratic-Republicans (or later Republicans). Hamilton's supporters were called Federalists.

By the election of 1792, both parties began to emerge. Washington was again elected unanimously, but the race for Vice-President between Adams (a Federalist) and George Clinton (a Democratic-Republican) was close. When Washington chose not to run for a third term in 1796, the stage was set for the true entry of party politics. The Federalists ran Adams and Thomas Pinckney. The Republicans ran Jefferson and Aaron Burr. It was thought that the electors would support both their candidates. But in the end it was Adams, the Federalist, who became President, and Jefferson, the Republican, who became Vice-President.

By 1800 Jefferson and Adams again opposed each other, and Burr was running against Pinckney for Vice-President. Everybody knew this, but this time the electors were very much pledged to their candidates. All 73 of the Republican electors voted for both Jefferson and Burr, the result being a tie. When there is a tie, the President is elected by the House of Representatives. It was quite clear that a pattern was emerging. Political parties, complete with party loyalty, were here to stay. The House was controlled by Federalists and they voted 35 times, always ending in a tie. Their leader Alexander Hamilton preferred Jefferson to Burr, so he used his influence on the 36th ballot to help Jefferson win. But the election showed that it was clearly time for a change in the method of electing our President. The 12th Amendment provided that change.

Name _____

THE BIRTH OF POLITICAL PARTIES

1. Describe both the pros and cons of having a President from one party and a Vice-President from another party.

   _____

   _____

   _____

   _____

2. Why did the emergence of political parties require that the manner of electing the President be changed?

   _____

   _____

   _____

   _____

   _____

   _____

3. Find out how Aaron Burr expressed his displeasure over the support Alexander Hamilton gave to Thomas Jefferson in the election of 1800.

   _____

   _____

   _____

   _____

4. Research the basic differences between the two major political parties today and briefly list those differences.

   _____

   _____

   _____

   _____

Looking back at... Amendments 11 and 12

1. What does the 11th Amendment say about cases filed by private citizens against states?

_____

2. What was the reason for Congress proposing the 11th Amendment which took away the federal court's right to hear a case filed by a private citizen of one state or a foreigner against another state?

_____

3. Comparing the methods of electing the President under Article 2, who chose the President?

_____

Under the 12th Amendment, who chooses the President?

_____

4. Under Article 2, who chose the electors?

_____

5. Under the present system (12th Amendment) who chooses the electors?

_____

6. Under Article 2, how did a candidate become President?

_____

_____

7. Under the present system, how does a candidate win the presidency?

_____

_____

8. Under Article 2, how was the Vice-President chosen?

_____

_____

9. How did the 12th Amendment change the way the Vice-President is chosen?

_____

ELECTION DAY

The procedure for presidential elections today has each major party presenting a ticket that includes both a presidential candidate and a vice-presidential candidate. The two run as a team. When the people vote, they make their choice from either the Democratic presidential candidate and vice-presidential candidate *or* the Republican presidential candidate and vice-presidential candidate. People cannot vote for a presidential candidate from one party and a vice-presidential candidate from the other party. But as you learned earlier, the people do not directly elect their President and Vice-President. They are elected by the Electoral College, which is made up of all the electors from all the states. Each state has the same number of electors as it has representatives plus senators. For example, a state with 24 representatives would be entitled to 26 electoral votes (24, its number of representatives, plus 2, its number of senators). That state's major political parties would each choose 26 electors. The people chosen to serve as electors are usually good strong party members who have devoted many hours of service.

On election day the people then decide which set of candidates they prefer. This is called the "popular vote" of the people. At the end of the day the votes are all tallied up and whichever team of candidates has received the most popular votes in that state wins all of the electors in that state. It doesn't matter how close the popular vote is among the people. It's a winner-take-all in each state and in the nation's capital. We all usually know by the end of election night which candidate has won the most electoral votes and thus the presidency. But over a month later the winning set of electors in each state meets in their own respective state capitals, and they go through the formality of casting their electoral votes for the President (and Vice-President).

ELECTION DAY

1. The philosophy used by the authors of the Constitution in having the two best qualified men become President and Vice-President was a good one and it worked well for awhile. But what happened which caused the system to fall apart and bring about the 12th Amendment?

   _____

   _____

   _____

2. Go back to page 66 and look at the map of the United States. How many total electoral votes did you count in all the states and in Washington, D.C.?

   _____

   _____

3. What is the number of electoral votes each candidate is hoping to win on election night as he watches the results come in?

   _____

   _____

4. Look at the map again. Why is it good political strategy for candidates to spend much of their time and money campaigning in the states which have the most electoral votes?

   _____

   _____

5. List in descending order the ten states which have the most electoral votes. Indicate the number each of these states has. How many total electoral votes are represented by these ten states?

   _____

   _____

   _____

6. Why is three votes the smallest number of electors any state has?

   _____

   _____

IN THE WAKE OF WAR

These next three amendments (13, 14, 15) all deal with slavery and the treatment of the Blacks once they were set free. Throughout the early history of this country there had been debate and disagreement over the institution of slavery. When the framers of the Constitution came to the issue, there was so much disagreement that there was question of whether there would even be a Constitution.

So they resolved the issue temporarily through compromise and postponement. But the issue was not resolved peacefully, and the nation went to war with itself. Thousands of lives were lost, families were destroyed and much of the South was virtually destroyed in the Civil War. And one of our greatest Presidents was assassinated. The end result of it all, however, was that the slaves were set free. These amendments provided the constitutional groundwork for rebuilding the South.

Amendment 13

Section 1. Neither slavery nor involuntary servitude, except as a punishment for crime whereof the party shall have been duly convicted, shall exist within the United States, or any place subject to their jurisdiction.

Section 2. Congress shall have power to enforce this article by appropriate legislation.

The Abolition of Slavery

Slavery shall no longer be allowed in the United States or in any of the land under its jurisdiction. No man may be forced to do the work of another unless the courts decree such work as punishment for committing a crime. *Lincoln's Emancipation Proclamation technically freed all the slaves in the states that had left the Union and joined the Confederacy. And many slave owners had already freed their slaves during the War. But this constitutional amendment made it official that all practices associated with slavery would be forever abolished in the United States.*

Congress shall have the power to make laws that will make this amendment effective.

Amendment 14

Section 1. All persons born or naturalized in the United States, and subject to the jurisdiction thereof, are citizens of the United States and of the state wherein they reside. No state shall make or enforce any law which shall abridge the privileges or immunities of citizens of the United States; nor shall any state deprive any person of life, liberty, or property, without due process of law; nor deny to any person within its jurisdiction the equal protection of the laws.

Former Slaves Made Citizens

All people who are either born here or become naturalized in the United States and are subject to its laws are citizens of the United States. Such citizens are also citizens of the respective states in which they live, and the states cannot make or enforce laws that may deprive these people of enjoying their rights as U.S. citizens. Nor can states take away people's lives, their liberty or their property without due process of law. People who live in any of our states are entitled to the same protection and benefits enjoyed by all others who live in that state. *This section was cited often to help win cases filed by Blacks who were being discriminated against.*

Section 2. Representatives shall be apportioned among the several states according to their respective numbers, counting the whole number of persons in each state, excluding Indians not taxed. But when the right to vote at any election for the choice of electors for President and Vice-President of the United States, representatives in Congress, the executive and judicial officers of a state, or the members of the legislature thereof, is denied to any of the male inhabitants of such state, being twenty-one years of age, and citizens of the United States, or in any way abridged, except for participation in rebellion, or other crime, the basis of representation therein shall be reduced in the proportion which the number of such male citizens shall bear to the whole number of male citizens twenty-one years of age in such state.

The number of representatives in the House of Representatives allowed in each state shall be based on a count of all the people except the untaxed Indians. Any state who tries to keep male citizens, who are over twenty-one years of age and who have not been convicted of a crime, from voting in presidential elections shall have their representation in Congress cut proportionately. *This paragraph totally changed the "three-fifths" clause found in Section 2 of Article 1. It was also intended to force states to grant voting rights to black men who had been former slaves. But there was a great deal of prejudice and discrimination and denial to those people in the South, and the penalties threatening to reduce representation in Congress were never enforced.*

Section 3. No person shall be a senator or representative in Congress, or elector of President or Vice-President, or hold any office, civil or military, under the United States, or under any state, who, having previously taken an oath, as a member of Congress, or as any officer of the United States, or as a member of any state legislature, or as an executive or judicial officer of any state, to support the Constitution of the United States, shall have engaged in insurrection or rebellion against the same, or given aid or comfort to the enemies thereof. But Congress may by a vote of two-thirds of each house, remove such disability.

Anyone who was a member of Congress, or an elector or who held a civil or military office in one of the states that seceded from the United States during the Civil War shall not be allowed to vote nor hold public office. *This section was designed to punish the leaders of the Confederacy. It was removed in 1898 by Congress.*

Section 4. The validity of the public debt of the United States, authorized by law, including debts incurred for payment of pensions and bounties for services in suppressing insurrection or rebellion shall not be questioned. But neither the United States nor any state shall assume or pay any debt or obligation incurred in aid of insurrection or rebellion against the United States, or any claim for the loss of emancipation of any slave; but all such debts, obligations and claims shall be held illegal and void.

All debts and pensions and payments of the Union shall be honored and paid without question. All debts and pensions and payments accrued by those states in rebellion (the Confederacy) cannot and will not be paid by the federal government. Nor can any payments be made for those slaves.

Section 5. The Congress shall have power to enforce, by appropriate legislation, the provisions of this article.

Congress has the power to make laws that will enforce the statements made in this amendment.

Amendment 15

Blacks Given the Right to Vote

Section 1. The right of citizens of the United States to vote shall not be denied or abridged by the United States or by any state on account of race, color, or previous condition of *servitude.*

The right of citizens of the United States to vote shall not be denied by the United States nor by any state because of race, color or because of past service as a slave.

Section 2. The Congress shall have power to enforce this article by appropriate legislation.

Congress has the power to make laws that will enforce the statements made in this amendment.

Name _____

THE END OF SLAVERY

1. What is the lone exception to the statement that involuntary servitude "shall not be permitted in our society"?

   _____

   _____

2. What are the two methods of gaining citizenship here in the United States?

   _____

   _____

   _____

3. What is the main intention of the 14th Amendment?

   _____

   _____

4. How does the 14th Amendment, Section 2, change the census from the way in which it was to be taken according to Article 1, Section 2?

   _____

   _____

5. According to the 14th Amendment, what would be the qualifications for voting?

   _____

   _____

6. What was to be the penalty imposed on a state that would deny qualified voters their legal right to vote?

   _____

   _____

   _____

7. According to the 14th Amendment, no person shall hold a government office who once took an oath of office swearing to uphold the Constitution, and then engaged himself in a rebellion against the United States. This section took away many good leaders from the South and created a situation of corrupt government when certain "carpetbaggers" from the North rushed to the South to claim the political positions made available by the rule. This restriction against leaders of the South became known as the *Black Code.* Such restrictions could only be removed by a _____ vote of the members of Congress. This was finally done in 1898.

8. Reread Section 4 of the 14th Amendment. What do you find to be the major difference in the way war debts of the South were to be treated as compared to the war debts of the North?

_____

_____

_____

9. The 14th Amendment made Blacks citizens and also outlined requirements for voting (which included Blacks). Why then, do you suppose Congress felt the need for the 15th Amendment?

_____

_____

_____

10. Why did the 15th Amendment not come right out and say that Blacks could vote, rather than using the words: "No one can be denied the right to vote because of his race, his sex, his color, or because he was once a slave"?

_____

_____

11. Based on what you've learned from the 14th Amendment, develop an explanation for the reasons there was still hatred between the North and South long after the war was over.

_____

_____

_____

Amendment 16

The Congress shall have power to lay and collect taxes on incomes, from whatever source derived, without apportionment among the several states, and without regard to any census or enumeration.

Income Tax

Congress shall have the power to assess a tax on all individual incomes, regardless of the sources from which they come. The amount of money collected will not be divided equally among the states nor the people. *Prior to the 16th Amendment, the federal government relied mostly on tariffs and excise taxes to support its functions financially. Taxes assessed on individual incomes would provide the government much more money. Those who supported the amendment justified their feelings on the grounds that everyone should pay support for his government according to his ability to pay.*

Many people have had many different ideas down through the years. Discuss what is wrong with this "fair-to-all" plan. Figure out how much money the federal government is going to need in a given year. Then divide that amount by 50 (because there are 50 states). Then have each state divide its "fair" share by the number of people who live in that state.

_____

_____

_____

_____

There have been many attempts down through the years to reform the federal income tax to plug up many of the loopholes and make it more fair to all. Perhaps the best to date was the 1986 tax reform under President Reagan. Research that plan and briefly discuss below the reasons why it seems more fair than any of our previous tax reform plans.

_____

_____

_____

_____

Amendment 17

The Senate of the United States shall be composed of two senators from each state, elected by the people thereof, for six years; and each senator shall have one vote. The electors in each state shall have the qualifications requisite for electors of the most numerous branch of the state legislatures.

When vacancies happen in the representation of any state in the Senate, the executive authority of such state shall issue writs of election to fill such vacancies: *Provided,* That the legislature of any state may empower the executive thereof to make temporary appointments until the people fill the vacancies by election as the legislature may direct.

This amendment shall not be so construed as to affect the election or term of any senator chosen before it becomes valid as part of the Constitution.

Direct Election of Senators

The Senate shall consist of two senators from each state, elected by the people for six-year terms. Each senator shall have one vote. Those who are qualified to vote for the largest house in their own state legislature may also vote for the two senators who serve their state.

Whenever a vacancy shall occur in the Senate, the governor of the state affected shall call for a special election to fill that vacancy. However, the governor may be empowered by the state legislature to appoint a temporary replacement until the election is held.

This amendment shall not affect the election or term of office for anyone serving in the Senate at the time it becomes a part of the Constitution.

1. How did the 17th Amendment change the way U.S. senators were to be elected? ___

___

2. What are the two alternatives to filling a vacancy in the U.S. Senate? ___

___

Amendment 18

Prohibition

Section 1. After one year from the ratification of this article the manufacture, sale, or transportation of intoxicating liquors within, the importation thereof into, or the exportation thereof from the United States and all territory subject to the jurisdiction thereof for beverage purposes is hereby prohibited.

One year after ratification of this amendment, it became illegal to manufacture, sell or transport alcoholic liquors anywhere in the United States and its territories. It also became illegal to export alcoholic liquors out of the country or to import them into the United States or its territories.

Section 2. The Congress and the several states shall have concurrent power to enforce this article by appropriate legislation.

The Congress and the state legislatures shall share in the power to enforce this amendment through appropriate legislation. *The Volstead Act passed by Congress provided most of the specific law needed to put teeth into the amendment and define the penalties for violating the law.*

Section 3. This article shall be inoperative unless it shall have been ratified as an amendment to the Constitution by the legislatures of the several states, as provided in the Constitution, within seven years from the date of the submission hereof to the states by the Congress.

This amendment shall not become effective unless it is ratified by three-fourths of the state legislatures within seven years from the date of its submission to the state by Congress. *Beginning with this amendment, it became common practice to allow a period of seven years between proposal and ratification. If a proposed amendment did not receive proper ratification within that time period, then it would be dropped.*

How many state legislatures were required to ratify the 18th Amendment? (Be careful to note the date when it was ratified.) _____

Name _____

PROGRESSIVE ERA

The 18th Amendment was another result of the work of the Progressives who were also partially responsible for the 16th, 17th, and the 19th Amendments. Though those Progressives represented several different specific interest groups, there was a common thread that tied them all together. Read about the Progressive movement and discuss how the mood of the time period and the changes that were going on made it a perfect time in history for such legislation. Also define this common thread that linked all the Progressives to a common goal.

Amendment 19

The right of citizens of the United States to vote shall not be denied or abridged by the United States or by any state on account of sex.

Congress shall have power to enforce this article by appropriate legislation.

Women Suffrage

The right of citizens of the United States to vote cannot be denied by the United States nor by any state because of sex.

Congress has the power to make laws that will enforce this amendment. *Suffrage is defined as the privilege of voting.*

WOMEN SUFFRAGE

The campaign of women to win the right to vote began in the 1840's. At first it was met with a great deal of antagonism. During the 1880's and 1890's, the movement began to lose its steam, and it wasn't until the early 1900's that it was revived again, this time with renewed enthusiasm. One of its strongest supporters was Susan B. Anthony. In fact the 19th Amendment is often called the "Susan B. Anthony Amendment." Find a biographical sketch of this great champion of women's rights and answer the following:

1. Who was Susan B. Anthony's close friend and associate who helped carry the flag through many of the campaigns waged to improve the rights of women?

   _____

2. Susan B. Anthony is perhaps best remembered as the pioneer of rights for women. But there were other areas of reform for which she also worked very hard. What were her other "causes"?

   _____

   _____

   _____

   _____

   _____

3. Why did Miss Anthony never enjoy the privilege afforded women by the 19th Amendment?

   _____

   _____

   _____

4. What percentage of the voting public was represented by women in the last presidential election?

   _____

5. How important is it for those who run for President to win the votes of women?

   _____

   _____

   _____

   _____

Amendment 20—Lame Duck Amendment

Under the original Constitution, the newly elected President took over his office on March 4 (four months) following the November election. Newly elected members had to wait until the next December (thirteen months) before the next session of Congress began. Between the time of election and the time when the new President and members of Congress took office, the old President and members of Congress continued in office. This time period between was called a "lame duck" time because those who had either been voted out of office or chose not to run for reelection were said to be lame ducks. They were virtually powerless, and the country lacked solid leadership during this period. The main purpose of the 20th Amendment was to shorten that period between election day and the time when the newly elected President and members of Congress took office.

Section 1. The terms of the President and Vice-President shall end at noon on the twentieth day of January, and the terms of senators and representatives at noon on the third day of January, of the years in which such terms would have ended if this article had not been ratified; and the terms of their successors shall then begin.

The terms of office for the President and the Vice-President shall end at noon on January 20; and the terms of office for senators and representatives shall end at noon on January 3. These terms end in the same year they would have ended if this amendment had not been ratified, and the terms of their successors shall begin at that time.

Section 2. The Congress shall assemble at least once in every year, and such meetings shall begin at noon on the third day of January, unless they shall by law appoint a different day.

Congress shall meet at least once every year, beginning at noon on January 3, unless Congress chooses a different day to begin its meetings. *This session begins on January 3, but continues open all year long with the exception of weekends and occasional recesses as chosen by the Congress. It may also choose to adjust its opening if January 3 should fall on a weekend.*

Section 3. If, at the time fixed for the beginning of the term of the President, the President-elect shall have died, the Vice-President-elect shall become President. If a President shall not have been chosen before the time fixed for the beginning of his term, or if the President-elect shall have failed to qualify, then the Vice-President-elect shall act as President until a President shall have qualified; and the Congress may by law provide for the case wherein neither a President-elect nor a Vice-President-elect shall have qualified, declaring who shall then act as President, or the manner in which one who is to act shall be selected, and such person shall act accordingly until a President or Vice-President shall have qualified.

Section 4. The Congress may by law provide for the case of the death of any of the persons from whom the House of Representatives may choose a President whenever the right of choice shall have devolved upon them, and for the case of the death of any of the persons from whom the Senate may choose a Vice-President whenever the right of choice shall have devolved upon them.

Section 5. Sections 1 and 2 shall take effect on the fifteenth day of October following the ratification of this article.

Section 6. This article shall be inoperative unless it shall have been ratified as an amendment to the Constitution by the legislatures of three-fourths of the several states within seven years from the date of its submission.

If the President-elect should die before actually assuming the office, then the Vice-President-elect shall become President. If a President has not been chosen by January 20, or if the person chosen should fail to qualify, then the Vice-President-elect shall fill in as the President until one is chosen. Congress can pass a law to decide who shall act as President if no one has been officially elected as President or as Vice-President. The person so designated shall serve only until a President or Vice-President is properly elected.

Congress shall have the power to make a law to determine what to do in the case of the House of Representatives having to elect the President and that chosen person dying before he assumes office. Congress also has the power to decide what shall be done in the event that the Senate must choose a Vice-President and that person dies before assuming office.

Sections 1 and 2 shall take effect on the fifteenth of October that follows proper ratification of this amendment.

This amendment shall be dropped if it has not been ratified by three-fourths of the state legislatures within seven years of its formal proposal.

LAME DUCK AMENDMENT

1. How often is Congress required constitutionally to meet?

   _____

2. How is the lame duck period shortened by the 20th Amendment? Compare the period prior to the 20th Amendment to the way it is today.

   _____

   _____

   _____

3. Reread the 20th Amendment. What will happen if the House of Representatives is forced to elect the President and their choice should die before assuming office?

   _____

   _____

   _____

   _____

4. What are some reasons you can think of for the period between the time of election and assumption of office being called "lame duck"?

   _____

   _____

   _____

   _____

   _____

   _____

The 18th Amendment was one of those ratified during the Progressive movement. While their strength in numbers and well-planned strategies were effective in implementing the public pressure needed to get the amendment ratified, the validity of the amendment itself lay in getting the American public to abide by its rules. And here the amendment was a miserable failure. On the one hand, there weren't enough agents to enforce the Volstead Act. On the other, the Americans did not want to be told what to do. They had just survived the "war-to-end-all-wars" (World War I). Men had laid their lives on the line and survived. Others had made great sacrifices here at home. With the war over, there was a feeling of optimism in the air, and it became a time of carefree living. A party atmosphere with dancing and drinking and fun-loving good times was more the order of the day.

With the taverns and nightclubs closed down, Americans began to gather together in illegal clubs called *speakeasies.* There people could get liquor made illegally here in the United States or smuggled in from abroad. This *bootlegging* and illegal traffic in liquor was highly profitable to those who dared to participate, and the competition over this illegal trade soon spawned a great deal of crime and violence. The entire moral fiber of the nation began to deteriorate. The "noble experiment" had failed. To bring an end to the failure, the 18th Amendment was repealed by the 21st Amendment.

Amendment 21

Section 1. The eighteenth article of amendment to the Constitution of the United States is hereby repealed.

Section 2. The transportation or importation into any state, territory, or possession of the United States for delivery or use therein of intoxicating liquors, in violation of the laws thereof, is hereby prohibited.

Section 3. This article shall be inoperative unless it shall have been ratified as an amendment to the Constitution by conventions in the several states, as provided in the Constitution, within seven years from the date of the submission hereof to the states by the Congress.

The Repeal of Prohibition

The 18th Amendment to the Constitution is hereby repealed. Prohibition is no longer a part of federal laws.

The transporting or importing of alcohol into any state which prohibits liquor is against federal laws, too. *Even though Prohibition was outlawed at the national level, the amendment still recognized the rights of individual states to remain "dry."*

This amendment shall be inoperative if it is not ratifed by special conventions in three-fourths of the states within seven years of the date of its formal proposal. *Congress decided to place this amendment before special state conventions for ratification rather than allow the state legislatures to decide as they had all other proposed amendments. It didn't take long. In less than eight months, conventions had ratified the amendment in enough states to make it law, and thus undo what the 18th Amendment had done.*

REPEAL OF PROHIBITION—AMENDMENT 21

1. Why was the "noble experiment" (the 18th Amendment) such a failure in reality?

   _____

   _____

   What factors helped to contribute to its downfall?

   _____

   _____

   _____

2. Although Article 5 of the Constitution provides for two methods in ratifying amendments, the 21st Amendment is the only one to be ratified by special conventions held in the various states. All of the other twenty-five were ratified by the state legislatures. Why did Congress decide to have this one ratified through special convention?

   _____

   _____

   _____

3. The Prohibitionist movement never completely died, even though alcohol was made legal again by the 21st Amendment. The Prohibitionist party remains the third oldest political party in the United States. Although it never wins any offices, its candidates always claim a sprinkling of votes during each presidential election. Find out what the party stands for other than just banning the sale and use of alcohol.

   _____

   _____

   _____

   _____

   _____

The 22nd Amendment was prompted by Americans who questioned the length of time a President should serve. Prior to 1940 Presidents had served only one or two terms of office. But in 1940 Franklin D. Roosevelt was elected a third time and in 1944 ran again and won. Many Americans felt this was too long for one man to serve. The result was the 22nd Amendment.

Amendment 22

Section 1. No person shall be elected to the office of the President more than twice, and no person who has held the office of President, or acted as President, for more than two years of a term to which some other person was elected President shall be elected to the office of the President more than once. But this article shall not apply to any person holding the office of President when this article was proposed by the Congress, and shall not prevent any person who may be holding the office of President, or acting as President, during the term within which this article becomes operative from holding the office of President or acting as President during the remainder of such term.

Section 2. This article shall be inoperative unless it shall have been ratified as an amendment to the Constitution by the legislatures of three-fourths of the several states within seven years from the date of its submission to the states by the Congress.

President's Term of Office

No person can be elected to the office of the President more than twice, and anyone who has served in the capacity of President for more than two years of someone else's term can only be elected once. But this article does not apply to the person holding office at the time of its proposal (Harry Truman), nor will it affect the President in office or person holding the office at the time of its ratification. *Thus ten years is the maximum amount of time any single individual can serve as President. Conceivably someone who served as Vice-President could become President (if the office were to be vacated) and serve out the two years or less remaining on that term of office—then be elected President twice in his own right. But if the unexpired term he fulfilled was for longer than two years, then he could be elected only once.*

This amendment will be dropped if it is not properly ratified within seven years of the time of its formal proposal.

Looking back at... the 22nd Amendment

1. Which President led to the adoption of the 22nd Amendment and why was it added as a change in the Constitution?

   _____

   _____

2. Who was the first President to be affected by the rules as described in the 22nd Amendment?

3. If the term of office for a U.S. President is four years and a President can only serve two terms in office, explain how a President could conceivably serve as President for ten years.

   _____

   _____

4. On December 6, 1973, Gerald Ford was named Vice-President by President Nixon when the then Vice-President Spiro Agnew resigned. On August 9, 1974, President Nixon resigned from the presidency and Gerald Ford became President. Could Gerald Ford have sought the presidency himself in the election of 1976? Could Ford have run again in 1980?

   _____

   _____

5. There are both pros and cons to having a national leader serve as head of his country for an extended period of time. Discuss both arguments and decide which you think is best. Justify your answer.

   _____

   _____

   _____

   _____

★ ★ ★

Because the nation's capital, Washington, D.C., was not a part of any state, its citizens were not allowed to vote for their President. Neither did they have any representation in Congress. The 23rd Amendment did provide them with a method to vote for their President and Vice-President, but they still don't have true representation in Congress. The city is allowed one nonvoting member to sit in the House of Representatives, but he can only voice his opinion.

Amendment 23

Section 1. The district constituting the seat of government of the United States shall appoint in such manner as the Congress may direct:

A number of electors of President and Vice-President equal to the whole number of senators and representatives in Congress to which the District would be entitled if it were a state, but in no event more than the least populous state; they shall be in addition to those appointed by the states, but they shall be considered, for the purposes of the election of President and Vice-President, to be electors appointed by a state; and they shall meet in the district and perform such duties as provided by the twelfth article of amendment.

Section 2. The Congress shall have power to enforce this article by appropriate legislation.

Electoral Votes for Washington

The District of Columbia (Washington, D.C.) shall be allowed the same number of electors as it would have if it were a state, but that number cannot exceed the least populous state. The electors chosen to represent the District of Columbia shall follow the same rules and perform the same duties as the electors of the states as set forth in the 12th Amendment. *Although Washington, D.C., has a population of more than twice the size of the entire state of Alaska, the amendment restricts the city to three electors.*

Congress shall have the power to make laws to enforce the amendment.

Name _____

1. How does it happen that the nation's capital has three electoral votes?

_____

_____

2. With the 23rd Amendment, how many total electors are there in the Electoral College?

_____

3. How many electors does it take to win the presidency?

_____

Amendment 24

Poll Tax Abolished

Section 1. The right of citizens of the United States to vote in any primary or other election for President or Vice-President, for electors for President or Vice-President, or for senator or representative in Congress, shall not be denied or abridged by the United States or any state by reason of failure to pay any *poll tax* or other tax.

The right of citizens to vote in primary or other elections for President, Vice-President, senators or representatives shall not be denied by the United States nor by any state because of a failure to pay a poll tax. *Some states had discriminated against Blacks and poor whites by requiring voters to pay a tax to vote called a poll tax. This amendment outlawed such taxes at the national level. States were allowed to assess poll taxes on state elections, but they were discouraged because oftentimes national officials would be elected in the same election.*

Section 2. The Congress shall have the power to enforce this article by appropriate legislation.

Congress shall have the power to make laws to enforce this amendment.

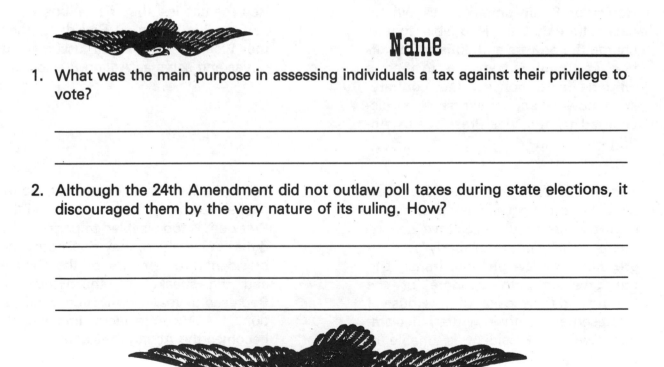

Name _____

1. What was the main purpose in assessing individuals a tax against their privilege to vote?

   _____

   _____

2. Although the 24th Amendment did not outlaw poll taxes during state elections, it discouraged them by the very nature of its ruling. How?

   _____

   _____

   _____

Amendment 25—Presidential Disability and Succession

The 25th Amendment became a part of the Constitution as a result of there being no plan under the original Constitution to provide for a Vice-President when the Vice-President moved up to fill a vacancy in the presidency. It also provided for a smooth transition for times when the Vice-President needs to take over for the President temporarily.

Section 1. In case of the removal of the President from office or his death or resignation, the Vice-President shall become President.

If the President is removed from office or dies or resigns, the Vice-President becomes President.

Section 2. Whenever there is a vacancy in the office of the Vice-President, the President shall nominate a Vice-President who shall take office upon confirmation by a majority vote of both houses of Congress.

When there occurs a vacancy in the office of the Vice-President, the President shall appoint someone who will take the office upon approval by a majority of both houses of Congress.

Section 3. Whenever the President transmits to the president pro tempore of the Senate and the speaker of the House of Representatives his written declaration that he is unable to discharge the powers and duties of his office, and until he transmits to them a written declaration to the contrary, such powers and duties shall be discharged by the Vice-President as Acting President.

When the President notifies in writing the president pro tempore of the Senate and the speaker of the House of Representatives that he is unable to perform his duties as President, then the Vice-President shall assume his duties and serve as Acting President.

Section 4. Whenever the Vice-President and a majority of either the principal officers of the executive departments or of such other body as Congress may by law provide, transmit to the president pro tempore of the Senate and the speaker of the House of Representatives their written declaration that the President is unable to discharge the powers and duties of his office the Vice-President shall immediately assume the powers and duties of the office as Acting President.

When the Vice-President and a majority of the members of the cabinet feel the President is too disabled to perform the duties of his office, they shall notify the president pro tempore of the Senate and the speaker of the House of Representatives. Upon such notification, the Vice-President immediately becomes the Acting President.

Thereafter, when the President transmits to the president pro tempore of the Senate and the speaker of the House of Representatives his written declaration that no inability exists, he shall resume the powers and duties of his office unless the Vice-President and a majority of either the principal officers of the executive departments or of such other body as Congress may by law provide, transmit within four days to the president pro tempore of the Senate and the speaker of the House of Representatives their written declaration that the President is unable to discharge the powers and duties of his office. Thereupon Congress shall decide the issue, assembling within forty-eight hours for that purpose if not in session. If the Congress, within twenty-one days after receipt of the latter written declaration, or, if Congress is not in session, within twenty-one days after Congress is required to assemble, determines by two-thirds vote of both houses that the President is unable to discharge the powers and duties of his office, the Vice-President shall continue to discharge the same as Acting President; otherwise, the President shall resume the powers and duties of his office.

When the President feels he has recovered from his disability or illness, he submits a written acknowledgment of such to the president pro tempore of the Senate and the speaker of the House of Representatives. If the Vice-President doesn't feel he has completely recovered, he must get agreement from a majority of the cabinet. If this occurs, notification is then sent on to the leaders of the two houses of Congress within four days. Congress then has 48 hours to assemble if its members are not in session and has 21 days to discuss the issues. It takes a two-thirds vote of both houses of Congress to keep the President from returning to his office. If two-thirds of both houses do agree that the President is still disabled, then the Vice-President shall continue acting as President.

Name _____

PRESIDENTIAL DISABILITY

1. The 25th Amendment was ratified in 1967. It was created as a result of the public concern over there being no Vice-President when Vice-President Lyndon Johnson became President after the assassination of John F. Kennedy. The amendment was used sooner than expected. Research its first use and explain the circumstances of how it led to a man becoming President of the United States without being elected.

_____

_____

_____

2. Under the terms described in the 25th Amendment, what would prevent an ambitious Vice-President from simply claiming the President "disabled" just to gain the office as Acting President?

_____

_____

3. When the President determines he is ready once again to assume his office, what steps are required of him?

_____

_____

4. We see several built-in measures in the 25th Amendment to prevent a President who is disabled from serving in our highest office. Who would be the best judge of whether or not a President is able to fulfill his duties as President?

_____

_____

Amendment 26

Section 1. The right of citizens of the United States, who are eighteen years of age or older, to vote shall not be denied or abridged by the United States or by any state on account of age.

Section 2. The Congress shall have power to enforce this article by appropriate legislation.

Eighteen-Year-Olds Vote

The right of citizens to vote who are eighteen years of age or older shall not be denied by the United States nor by any state because of age.

Congress shall have the power to enforce this amendment through appropriate legislation.

Name _____

1. Find out why the 26th Amendment became almost a necessity because of a ruling made by the Supreme Court upholding the Voting Rights Act.

   _____

   _____

   _____

   _____

2. There are still many people in the United States who feel that the voting age should be a minimum of 21 years. What do you think? Are 18-year-olds responsible enough to vote? What about 15-year-olds or 13-year-olds? What should the standards for voting be? Perhaps you have some other ideas. Discuss your thoughts and justify what you feel should be the requirements for voting here in the United States.

   _____

   _____

   _____

   _____

OUR AMENDMENTS AT WORK

Below are "living" examples of constitutional amendments at work. There is one situation that describes each of our 26 amendments so you'll have just enough to go around. Your task is to read each paragraph and then decide which constitutional amendment is at work. Place the number of that amendment in the blank space provided.

1. _____ Rasmusson is a legitimate, qualified law officer. He comes to the home of Johnson and demands entry into his house. Disregarding whether or not Johnson has something inside to hide, he tells Rasmusson to "Buzz off! You don't even have a search warrant." Which constitutional amendment allows Johnson this protection?

2. _____ Bradford Longhurst has the right to plan his family vacation to any place he wants to go. He wouldn't necessarily have this right in certain other countries of the world. Where in the Constitution does it say that Bradford has this right?

3. _____ Any black or member of any other minority who qualifies properly can vote in the USA because of this amendment. Which one is it?

4. _____ If either of the two U.S. senators from the state of Ohio should become incapable of performing his duties, then it would be up to the governor of Ohio to either find someone to take the place of the senator who vacated his office, or he could call for a special election. In which amendment is this provision found?

5. _____ Women are now allowed to vote just as men. Such was not always the case. In fact it took a constitutional amendment to win women the right to vote. This provision was made in which of the amendments?

6. _____ If Officer Hanson arrests Jackson for speeding and Jackson claims he is innocent, it then becomes Hanson's word against Jackson's (since Hanson was on his way home from work and did not have his radar gun). Jackson really believes he is innocent, but he figures the judge will probably believe Hanson because he is "on the side of the law." The penalty will be Jackson's third within a year; and as a result, he will lose his license for six months if he is found guilty. He does believe, however, that the judgment of twelve good people will decide in his favor; therefore, he demands a jury trial. Where in the Constitution is Jackson guaranteed this right?

7. _____ "I can say what I want, write what I want, worship as I please, call together a group of my friends to criticize the government; and I am also allowed to petition the proper authorities if I so desire." These rights that belong to us all are provided for in which of the amendments?

8. _____ Donahue and McMillan are at odds over the location of the boundary line dividing their properties. The area in question dates back to a mistake made when the land was originally surveyed and amounts to just under one-half acre altogether. Since the two can't agree on a settlement, they've decided to put the matter before a jury in a court of law. This they can do because of which constitutional amendment?

9. _____ In the election of 1800, history made it quite clear that the framers of the Constitution had made a mistake in having the Vice-President become the man who had the second highest number of votes for President. That was all changed in 1804 by what amendment?

10. _____ This amendment had the effect of cancelling the "three-fifths clause" (Article 1, Section 7, clause 3), which counted only three-fifths of the slaves for purposes of determining representation in Congress and taxation.

11. _____ Nate Williams is a poor black who lives in the state of Louisiana. A few years back Nate was not allowed to vote in state and local elections because he could not pay his poll tax. He couldn't afford to buy his right to vote because he considered food and shelter more important. He could, however, vote in national elections because of an amendment in the Constitution that forbids the use of a poll tax in national elections. Which one?

12. _____ Ronald Reagan became the nation's 40th President on Tuesday, January 20, 1981, at 12:00 noon EST. He was sworn into office by Chief Justice Warren Burger. Under the original Constitution, he would have had to wait until March 4 to take over as President. This lame duck amendment came to us through the ratification of which of our constitutional amendments?

13. _____ Gallagher was suspected and finally arrested for the murder of Silas McGee. There were no eyewitnesses to the shooting. Gallagher did have a motive, but he also has a fairly legitimate alibi that will explain his whereabouts at the time of the shooting. He tells his friend Herman Philpot that he isn't "really worried. There isn't enough evidence to even bring me to trial." He is right. The Grand Jury fails to find enough evidence against Gallagher to even bring him to trial, and he is released under a "no true bill" statement. This same right given to Gallagher is ensured to all of us because of which constitutional amendment?

14. _____ Henry Knott keeps a gun in his closet. Henry tells all of his friends that he keeps it there...not because he likes to hunt...but rather to "defend himself against anyone who would try to rob him." We all know that Henry could get himself into a whole lot of trouble if he uses that gun without caution. But on the other hand, we recognize Henry's right to keep the weapon to defend himself and that which is rightfully his. This right is one shared by all as a result of which of the constitutional amendments?

15. _____ As long as we enjoy domestic peace, we do not have to let soldiers live in our homes if we don't want them there. This privilege from being forced to quarter soldiers in our homes is all a part of which constitutional amendment?

16. _____ The power of Congress to levy a tax against the incomes of those who work in order to pay for the services of the federal government is clearly pointed out to us all in which amendment?

17. _____ Which of the amendments gives eighteen-year-olds the right to vote, a right that was formerly reserved for only those twenty-one years of age and older?

18. _____ The citizens of Washington, D.C., are now allowed to vote for their President, too. This right had been denied them before because only states were given electors, and the city of Washington, D.C., does not lie within the boundaries of any state. Which amendment changed all this to allow the citizens of our nation's capital the right to vote in presidential elections?

19. _____ Arnold Gross, formerly of Athens, Georgia, now living in Jackson, Mississippi, lodges a protest against the state of Georgia because he feels his business was unfairly taxed when he lived in Georgia. He even attempts to file a formal lawsuit against the state of Georgia. We all know that if the state of Georgia refuses to be sued by Mr. Gross, then poor Arnold is just out of luck because there is no place for the case to be heard. The plain fact of the matter is that the federal courts will not hear cases involving citizens of one state against another state. This is clearly pointed out in which of the constitutional amendments?

20. _____ Former President Nixon was elected twice by the people. Even though he resigned before his second term was finished, he could NOT have been elected to serve another term. Which of the constitutional amendments forbids a President from being elected to more than two terms of office?

21. _____ The rights of Americans to consume alcoholic beverages was taken away from them in 1919 by a constitutional amendment. However, because of public protest and because it was so very difficult to enforce, the amendment was later repealed. Which amendment attempted to stop Americans from drinking?

22. _____ We all know that it is now legal to consume alcoholic beverages so long as that person doing the drinking has satisfied the minimum age requirements. This right came to us only after the ratification of this amendment. It had the effect of undoing what an earlier amendment had done by banning the sale or consumption of liquor.

23. _____ An historical incident occurred not too long ago when Nelson Rockefeller was nominated by former President Ford and then confirmed as Vice-President by Congress. This action became necessary when former President Nixon resigned, thus leaving Vice-President Ford to succeed him as President. Vice-President Ford became Vice-President when he was appointed by President Nixon to fill the vacancy that had been created by the resignation of Spiro Agnew. There has since been provision made so that in the future there will always be a Vice-President. This provision became a reality because of which amendment?

24. _____ Clyde Billingsly is arrested for knocking down poor old Mrs. Finch (age 76) and then stealing her purse which contained $4.10. At the police station Clyde is treated rather harshly by the officers in charge and is bodily "thrown" into a cell. He overhears the arresting officer say that they are going to "throw the book" at him for doing such a lowly thing to such a nice little old lady. Clyde knows that he is a rascal, but he also chuckles at the comment because he knows that his penalty cannot be too harsh for committing such a minor offense as "purse snatching." Which amendment makes Clyde so certain?

25. _____ It became illegal for one man to hold another as a slave as a result of which constitutional amendment?

26. _____ The paragraph ensuring that all powers not delegated to the federal government are indeed "reserved for either the states or the people" is found in which constitutional amendment?

Looking back on... the Constitution

Name _____

Below are some statements about the Constitution which are not true. First read each statement; then locate the section and clause in the Constitution that pertains to that statement, and rewrite it so that it is true.

1. Congress has no right to meddle in the private affairs of the several states by controlling trade.

   Location: _____

   _____

   _____

2. Members of the House of Representatives are chosen by the voters every four years.

   Location: _____

   _____

   _____

3. The Congress must have approval from the President on all resolutions to make them take effect.

   Location: _____

   _____

   _____

4. It is not always necessary to have witnesses who speak against the accused in court.

   Location: _____

   _____

   _____

5. The term of office for a federal judge is ten years.

   Location: _____

   _____

   _____

6. All foreign ambassadors nominated by the President need approval by two-thirds of the Senate.

   Location: _____

   _____

7. If a majority of the Senate feels a disabled President is unable to return to his office, they must notify his cabinet.

   Location: _____

   _____

   _____

8. The President of the United States must be at least thirty years of age.

   Location: _____

   _____

   _____

9. If no candidate for President has a majority of the electors, the President is chosen by the cabinet.

   Location: _____

   _____

   _____

10. A fleeing criminal can escape justice by crossing into another state where he cannot be prosecuted.

    Location: _____

    _____

    _____

11. Congress has command over the nation's armed forces.

    Location: _____

    _____

    _____

12. Only authorized law enforcement officers have a right to own guns.

    Location: _____

    _____

    _____

13. The power of impeachment rests with a majority of both houses of Congress.

    Location: _____

    _____

    _____

14. No President can serve more than two terms or eight years.

    Location: _____

    _____

    _____

15. Exorbitant fines and punishments are only levied against third-time offenders.

    Location: _____

    _____

    _____

16. No person shall be convicted of treason without the testimony of an eyewitness to the act.

    Location: _____

    _____

    _____

17. New states can only be admitted to the Union by approval of the President and a vote of two-thirds of Congress.

    Location: _____

    _____

    _____

18. To amend the Constitution requires ratification by two-thirds of the state legislatures.

    Location: _____

    _____

    _____

19. The government cannot buy the land of those who do not wish to sell.

    Location: _____

    _____

    _____

20. Individual states can coin their own money only with the approval of Congress.

    Location: _____

    _____

    _____

WE THE PEOPLE

This exciting and challenging game for the entire class can provide the perfect finish to your units of study on our nation's most precious document. Most of the one hundred sixty trivia questions are based on the information presented in the text of the Constitution itself. But there are some that will surface as real challenges that can be answered only by those who involved themselves in research and discussion activities. There are four questions on each card for a total of forty game cards. The correct answer to each corresponding question is found on the back of the card. To ensure the durability of the game cards and to make them easier to handle, it is suggested that they be laminated or covered with clear Con-Tact paper before being cut apart. If the teacher wants the children to have advance practice time before playing the game, both sides of each card should be reproduced before the cards are cut apart.

To play the game, the class is divided into as many teams as desired, but three to five players per team usually work best. Order of play is determined by a roll of the die with the team having the highest roll going first. The cards are shuffled and a representative from the first team rolls the die. The top card is chosen and the teacher reads the numbered question on the card that corresponds to the number of spots showing on the die. If a five or a six is rolled, that player loses his turn. The members of that team then have ten seconds to report their answer. They may confer among themselves, but the first answer heard is the answer that must be used. If the answer is incorrect, the next team must answer the missed question.

The first team to score twenty points is declared the winning team. Fewer or more point goals may be used as time allows. A variation is to make questions in later rounds worth more points. If this is done, the winning goal should be adjusted accordingly. A spinner can be used in place of a die if desired. The game also becomes a useful learning tool for two children in a learning center. The same rules apply, but a quiet version involves a generic gameboard, a marker for each player and as many questions as needed to get the winner from *start* to *finish* on the gameboard.

Card 1

1. Our country's first framework of national government
2. The year our present Constitution was written
3. The city where the Constitution was written
4. The building where the Constitution was written

Card 2

1. Unlike Article 3 of the Constitution, the Articles of Confederation made no provisions for these.
2. Because the Articles of Confederation did not provide for a strong central government, this was written.
3. He presided over the Constitutional Convention.
4. He wrote the Constitution in its final form.

Card 3

1. The date when the Constitution was signed
2. The number of men who signed the original Constitution
3. The number of states represented at the Convention
4. The only state not represented at the Constitutional Convention

Card 4

1. The number of branches in our federal government
2. The legislative arm of our national government
3. The judicial part of our federal government
4. The leader of our executive department

Card 5

1. The number of amendments added to the Constitution under the Bill of Rights
2. The name given to the first ten amendments
3. The year the Constitution became the Law of the Land
4. They make our laws.

Card 6

1. The number of representatives in Congress
2. The number of representatives a state gets is determined by this.
3. The length of term of office for a U.S. representative
4. The title given those who serve in the House of Representatives

Card 7

1. The title given to those who serve in the U.S. Senate
2. The minimum age requirement for members of the House of Representatives
3. The frequency of our census
4. The title of the leader of the House of Representatives

Card 8

1. The minimum length of time as a U.S. citizen required of a member of the House of Representatives
2. They choose the speaker of the House.
3. The minimum number of representatives a state may have
4. They have the power of impeachment.

1. courts
2. Constitution
3. George Washington
4. Gouverneur Morris

1. Articles of Confederation
2. 1787
3. Philadelphia
4. Independence Hall

1. 3
2. Congress
3. U.S. courts
4. President

1. Sept. 17, 1787
2. 39
3. 12
4. Rhode Island

1. 435
2. population
3. 2 years
4. congressmen

1. 10
2. Bill of Rights
3. 1788
4. Congressmen

1. 7 years
2. House of Representatives
3. 1
4. House of Representatives

1. senators
2. 25
3. 10 years
4. speaker

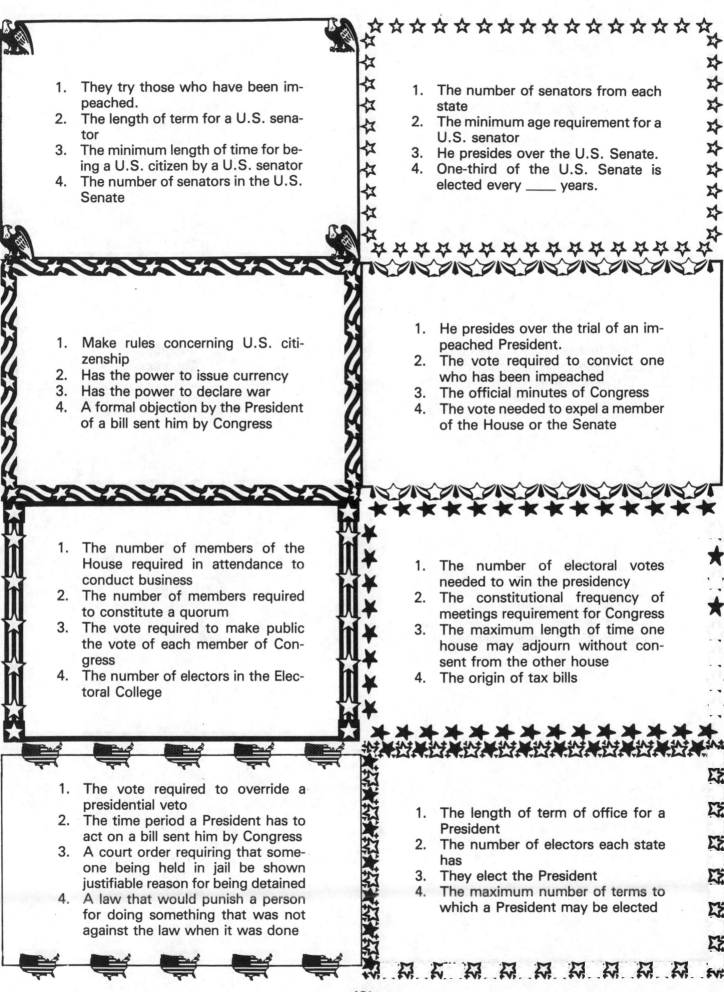

Box 1 (top left):

1. They try those who have been impeached.
2. The length of term for a U.S. senator
3. The minimum length of time for being a U.S. citizen by a U.S. senator
4. The number of senators in the U.S. Senate

Box 2 (top right):

1. The number of senators from each state
2. The minimum age requirement for a U.S. senator
3. He presides over the U.S. Senate.
4. One-third of the U.S. Senate is elected every ____ years.

Box 3 (middle left):

1. Make rules concerning U.S. citizenship
2. Has the power to issue currency
3. Has the power to declare war
4. A formal objection by the President of a bill sent him by Congress

Box 4 (middle right):

1. He presides over the trial of an impeached President.
2. The vote required to convict one who has been impeached
3. The official minutes of Congress
4. The vote needed to expel a member of the House or the Senate

Box 5 (lower middle left):

1. The number of members of the House required in attendance to conduct business
2. The number of members required to constitute a quorum
3. The vote required to make public the vote of each member of Congress
4. The number of electors in the Electoral College

Box 6 (lower middle right):

1. The number of electoral votes needed to win the presidency
2. The constitutional frequency of meetings requirement for Congress
3. The maximum length of time one house may adjourn without consent from the other house
4. The origin of tax bills

Box 7 (bottom left):

1. The vote required to override a presidential veto
2. The time period a President has to act on a bill sent him by Congress
3. A court order requiring that someone being held in jail be shown justifiable reason for being detained
4. A law that would punish a person for doing something that was not against the law when it was done

Box 8 (bottom right):

1. The length of term of office for a President
2. The number of electors each state has
3. They elect the President
4. The maximum number of terms to which a President may be elected

1. 2
2. 30
3. Vice-President
4. 2

1. Senate
2. 6 years
3. 9 years
4. 100

1. Chief Justice of the Supreme Court
2. 2/3 of the senators present
3. *Congressional Record*
4. 2/3

1. Congress
2. Congress
3. Congress
4. veto

1. 270
2. once each year
3. 3 days
4. House of Representatives

1. 218
2. 51
3. 1/5
4. 538

1. 4 years
2. its number of senators plus representatives
3. Electoral College
4. two

1. 2/3
2. 10 days
3. writ of habeas corpus
4. ex post facto law

1. He was and will always be the only President elected four times.
2. The longest a President can possibly serve
3. The age requirement for a U.S. President
4. The minimum number of years a U.S. President can live in the United States

1. Inauguration Day
2. He presides over the Senate in the absence of the Vice-President.
3. He shall take over for the President in the event the President cannot serve.
4. This office follows the Vice-President in the line of succession to the President.

1. Possesses the power to make treaties with foreign nations
2. The necessary approval to validate all foreign treaties
3. The power to nominate federal judges
4. The number of judges on the Supreme Court

1. The length of term of office for a U.S. judge
2. The date when Congress begins
3. The highest court in the judicial system
4. The power to admit states into the Union

1. The number of witnesses necessary to convict someone of treason
2. The court order allowing an authorized search of a person's home and property
3. Trial by jury is guaranteed to all by the _____ Amendment.
4. To become a part of the Constitution, an amendment must be ratified by what fraction of the state legislatures?

1. To propose a constitutional amendment requires what fraction of both houses of Congress?
2. An amendment may become a part of the Constitution if it gets approval by conventions in _____.
3. An amendment may be formally proposed by a special convention called by _____.
4. The change in the Constitution that allows the federal government to tax incomes

1. The time between the election of new officials and the time they take office
2. The title of the head judge on the Supreme Court
3. The name given to the judges on the Supreme Court
4. The length of time that most amendments now have to be ratified

1. The number of articles in the original Constitution
2. The number of amendments to the Constitution
3. Has the authority to recognize the government of a new nation
4. That part of the Constitution that allows a person the right not to testify against himself

1. January 20
2. president pro tempore
3. Vice-President
4. speaker of the House

1. Franklin D. Roosevelt
2. 10 years
3. 35 years
4. 14 years

1. life
2. January 3
3. Supreme Court
4. Congress

1. President
2. 2/3 of the senators present
3. President
4. 9

1. 2/3
2. 3/4 of the states
3. 2/3 of the states
4. 16th Amendment

1. 2
2. search warrant
3. 6th
4. 3/4

1. 7
2. 26
3. President
4. 5th Amendment

1. lame duck period
2. Chief Justice
3. justices
4. 7 years

1. The amendment that protects the voting rights of women
2. If no candidate for President wins a majority of the electors, who chooses the President?
3. If no candidate for Vice-President wins a majority of the electors, who chooses the Vice-President?
4. A system of government which separates the powers between the states and the central government is called a _____.

1. The President's group of chief advisors
2. How many positions are there in the President's cabinet?
3. The amendment which was later repealed
4. A court order requiring the appearance of a witness named by the defendant

1. The path to U.S. citizenship other than by birth
2. The system which has built-in safeguards against excessive power to any one branch of government
3. A proposed law
4. A formal written accusation issued by a grand jury

1. A less serious crime punishable by a short jail sentence or fine
2. Aiding the enemy or selling out the secrets of the United States
3. The number of persons on a petit jury
4. The vote needed by a petit jury to reach a decision

1. The vote needed by the Supreme Court to reach a decision
2. The amendment that allows us to bear arms to defend ourselves
3. Being tried twice for the same crime
4. The right of the government to take land from a private individual for the good of all

1. The jury that determines the guilt or innocence of the accused
2. The constitutional basis for free speech
3. The location of the full faith and credit clause
4. The constitutional amendment that freed the slaves

1. It outlawed the poll tax in national elections
2. An opening statement of purpose
3. The right to vote
4. Those powers specifically given Congress in Article 1, Section 8

1. The last paragraph of Article 1, Section 8, defining the indirect power of Congress
2. A veto of a bill by the President in which he does not have ten days to react
3. The length of time the President has to act on a bill passed by Congress
4. Standard procedures followed in a court of law

1. his cabinet
2. 12
3. 18th Amendment
4. subpoena

1. 19th
2. House of Representatives
3. Senate
4. federal system

1. misdemeanor
2. treason
3. 12
4. unanimcus, 12—0

1. naturalization
2. checks and balances
3. bill
4. indictment

1. petit jury
2. 1st Amendment
3. Article 4
4. 13th

1. simple majority, 5—4
2. 2nd
3. double jeopardy
4. eminent domain

1. implied powers
2. pocket veto
3. 10 days
4. due process

1. 24th Amendment
2. Preamble
3. suffrage
4. express powers

Box 1 (top left)

1. Money provided by the accused to ensure his appearance in court
2. The source of the punishment must be appropriate to the crime committed.
3. The constitutional justification for allowing 18-year-olds the right to vote
4. The first President to be affected by the amendment which ensures that there will always be a Vice-President

Box 2 (top right)

1. The source of the right to a trial by jury if the value of the disputed property exceeds $20
2. This amendment made citizens of former slaves and protected their rights.
3. This amendment was meant to punish the south for leaving the Union.
4. The minimum number of presidential electors for a state

Box 3 (second row left)

1. The number of electors given to Washington, D.C., by the 23rd Amendment
2. It repealed Prohibition.
3. The legal term for going broke
4. Written letters of permission given to privateers allowing them to capture enemy ships and keep the cargo

Box 4 (second row right)

1. Legal document that protects the rights of an owner's invention
2. The number of electors for a state with 23 representatives
3. Legal protection of ownership to those who write songs
4. The source of the rule against quartering soldiers in private homes

Box 5 (third row left)

1. The constitutional amendment that gave the freed slaves the right to vote
2. The lame duck amendment
3. He is history's main source of information on the Constitution.
4. This amendment had the effect of cancelling the three-fifths clause.

Box 6 (third row right)

1. The amendment which prevented citizens of other states from suing a state in federal court
2. The President's role as head of the military
3. The President's annual message to the Congress and the people
4. The location of the "elastic clause"

Box 7 (bottom left)

1. The residence requirement for those seeking naturalization
2. The ceremony of installing the President in office
3. A law that singles out and punishes a single person considered an undesirable
4. The secret to the Constitutional Convention's success, i.e., each side was willing to give in to its demands for the good of all

Box 8 (bottom right)

1. Request to have an accused criminal returned to a state to face justice
2. The location of the national supremacy clause
3. The President's chief advisor on matters concerning America's public lands
4. The vote needed to approve the President's nomination of a foreign ambassador

1. 7th Amendment
2. 14th Amendment
3. 14th Amendment
4. 3

1. bail
2. 8th Amendment
3. 26th Amendment
4. Richard Nixon

1. patent
2. 25
3. copyright
4. 3rd Amendment

1. 3
2. 21st Amendment
3. bankruptcy
4. letters of marque

1. 11th Amendment
2. Commander in Chief
3. State of the Union message
4. Article 1, Section 8, clause 18

1. 15th Amendment
2. 20th Amendment
3. James Madison
4. 14th

1. extradition
2. Article 6
3. Secretary of Interior
4. simple majority of the Senate

1. 5 years
2. inauguration
3. bill of attainder
4. compromise

ANSWER KEY

Remembering Key Phrases   Page 11

1.	b	8.	a
2.	d	9.	e
3.	a	10.	a
4.	a	11.	a
5.	c	12.	b
6.	b	13.	c
7.	d	14.	e
		15.	a

We Hold These Truths . . .   Page 12

1.	e	8.	k
2.	c	9.	f
3.	n	10.	d
4.	j	11.	h
5.	i	12.	o
6.	m	13.	l
7.	b	14.	a
		15.	g

Our Basic Human Rights   Page 13

1. The rights to continue living, to be free, and to pursue that which makes us happy so long as we do not violate the rights of others
2. The committee felt they would only get in each other's way if they tried to write it together. So they assigned Jefferson the task of drafting the document, indicating they would react when he was finished. When he was done, very few suggestions were made.
3. Whenever repeated violation of human rights and serious injustices are committed against the people; when the people have appealed to their government for a correction of their injustices without response
4. From the power and with the consent of the people themselves

Page 14

5. Answers will vary.
6. That those who signed the Declaration would be marked men with the British. They needed to ally themselves together for their own protection.
7. He said he signed his name large enough so that King George would not have to use his bifocals to see it. The bold style in which he signed his name has become famous most probably because of the importance of the document he signed.

Looking back at . . . the Background   Page 21

1. Farmers were unhappy over farm prices. They sought help from the national government. The government could offer no help because it had very little power. Other problems were caused by this same lack of power.
2. Weak central government, no power to tax, no power to regulate trade, no power to coin money and back it up with previous standard, no money to raise an army or navy, no federal court system, no power to enforce the laws it did make.

Page 22

3. The larger states felt that since they had more people they should have more representation in the lawmaking body (Virginia Plan). The smaller states feared being dominated and thus wanted equal representation in all states (New Jersey Plan). The matter was solved with The Great Compromise—a Congress composed of both a house based on representation and a house where representation is equal.
4. Southern states wanted slaves counted as population when it came to determining representation, but they wanted to regard them as property for purposes of taxation to keep their state assessments lower. The three-fifths clause provided that three out of every five slaves would be counted in the population, both for determining representation and taxation.

Page 23

5. The basic framework and principles remain the same as they have for 200 years. The changes (after the Bill of Rights) reflect social values that have changed through the years.
6. The states were unwilling to give up their own individual powers under the Articles of Confederation, thus making them weak and ineffective.
7. It feared the Convention would take away its power to tax goods that passed through the state.

Page 24

8. Almost all of the leaders of the day were men of note who had distinguished themselves through achievement. Financial success usually went along with the acclaim.
9. They figured there would be enough divided issues that whatever compromises were eventually made would have a better chance of passing if the entire document were to be presented at one time in its final form.

Drawing Conclusions   Page 25

1.	F	6.	T
2.	T	7.	T
3.	T	8.	F
4.	T	9.	T
5.	F	10.	F

Preamble Scramble   Page 27

```
T WE THE PEOPLE R V W I T E R P S R T O F D O M N U X Y M
O R M T H Z Q O P S O O I H M N T D S O K R A B C Z P E P F Q O R
E T I N U F O E H T F F T H E U S T S O C P F E H R T O I R M V
P E R F E C T U S K T B A N R E L T A A B A K C A B F Y A N V A S
T E W O H A P N T M H A N A P U B A L S K O C D T U F B R E W Y M
R L T M T S M I A V E U N I T E D T U P N E I R F T S E B Y R E V
Q F S P Y B O O R O H L I T D O S E A T E S O F B E F R E I A N E
E S O S R U R N S I E A H W I N G S C O M E S A S T O T S A J R O
E R O M A M R O F O T R E D R O N I A C I R E M I H S I N E R G G
P R U S N I N N A T S E Z H T W Z I L A R O N M M E S T N I V R B
E R F E C T U T L I S H J U S T I C E I N O N E O L T I C A T I S
E D O M E S N E B W O N T H Y B F L D N S U R E D G C C T O T U O
L V Q C I T I V A F D N O M Y A R O O V A P A B A G N T O M H E I
I I N A R T O V T L S O P O M O R G F O R R H L T S E R F E D I D
T Y A F D N N E S O Y D O T M A P T H O F F S I T R Y A N Q U I L
S R T N A U S A I T S U P E P I E R E E O R T Y H E E A R S M A I
D E H O Y S T P S H T J E T E A S G N O M M O C E H T R O F D R T
A F L E W L A R E N E G E H N I N T D T E L H V S I T T R E N I Y
O A N C E M W E H I W M I F E F E N T B I A G N O S E D A O P
D R E H W I H N E R N T H E P O R L A D W T S D A D A T T I V O R
O E N V O I H T N A C H E L L P E D U H O I F Y A R P E Y F T Y H
U A N D H T E M N N G S O F O D D R N E K C I G D S R N I F A T E
T T V S S T I H T I N H I L B V T S E L V E S A N D A I T Y D O O
I J E E M T G P V S L H M I I T U R B T C M E N T O V R S I S A R
S U T C T H T U V S E T I B H H O U E T D U D H S U I E O N I T D
T J D U S V O P O E M H N E T G M O J R E L P R E R L T H T E C A
G E N R E T H E B L V M O R T Y T O V D A D N A R P O S E N R O I
E R A C O N S T I T U T I O N F O R T H H S I L B A T S E D N A N
E D L A R A S A C I V M O T S T I N V H T P V O A H E M A U T N E
F A N Y A S L G E L G I L O L M O S S O H I S C O N S T I T U T I
G R O A G T F O H O C N K D D O R F A F H T H O Y T N I C S D C O
N T U N D A C I R E M A F O S E T A T S D E T I N U E H T R O F N
C E I H A D F O T W E N T O S T O L L C C S T R I N G J S A T O U
```

Looking back at . . . Membership in Congress   Page 32

1. Article 1 clearly outlines the legislative branch of our government.
2. The legislative department makes the laws.
3. House of Representatives and the U.S. Senate
4. Congress
5.

House	Senate
25 years old	30 years old
7 years	9 years
live in congressional district	live in state
2 years	6 years
438 members	100 members

6. speaker; answers will vary.
7. Vice-President; answers will vary.

Page 33

8. The number of people in the state; answers will vary.
9. Governor either calls for a special election or appoints someone to serve until the next general election.
10. There was a great deal of controversy between the more populous states and the smaller states at the time the Constitution was written concerning how members of the legislature would be chosen. The smaller states wanted equal representation; the larger states wanted representation based on population. The issue was finally decided by having both.
11. Senate; equal representation
12. House of Representatives; more people would mean more representation.
13. To provide a way to remove those in positions of trust who would misuse their power for their own gain. The power was given to Congress to serve as a check in power on the other two branches of governement—namely executive and judicial. The House stands as the accuser; the Senate conducts the trial.

Page 34

14. simple majority; 2/3
15. Andrew Johnson
16. He was censured for attempting to fire one of Lincoln's cabinet members. Johnson was saved from conviction by one vote in the Senate.
17. Because the Vice-President who would normally be presiding over the trial would be next in line for the presidency, should the President be convicted
18. He was accused in the Watergate scandal of breaking into Democratic headquarters to discover political plans and strategies. He resigned from office once the House Judiciary committee made its recommendation to impeach him. This avoided the issue ever coming to a vote.

Page 35

19. Answers will vary.
20. Answers will vary.

Looking back on . . . Article I, Sections 4-6 — Page 38

1. The Tuesday after the first Monday in November of all even numbered years
2. Answers will vary.
3. January 3
4. To ensure that all voting is kept secret
5. simple majority; 220 in the House; 51 in the Senate
6. 2/3; 292; 67

Page 39

7. Though it doesn't sound fair, the House members would probably have access to any evidence of wrongdoing against the candidate that the public might not have.
8. 1/5
9. These men and women are the people *we* elected to make our laws. We have a right to know how they vote on laws that affect our interests and well-being. If we see they are not voting the way we like, we don't have to vote for them in the next election.
10. *Congressional Record*
11. 3 days
12. Both are required to pass legislation. The work of one house would be ineffective if the other was not in session.
13. They would have to answer to the people who pay their salaries—namely the taxpayers, the people who voted them into office.
14. To allow them the freedom to do their jobs. The paragraph has its roots etched in the days of Colonial America when King George's men would falsely detain those they considered threats on trumped-up charges, merely to keep them from causing trouble. The framers of the Constitution wanted its lawmakers to have the freedom to do what should be done.
15. It would be a position created while he was in office, thus he would be gaining from his own position as a congressman and this is forbidden in Article 1, Section 6, clause 2.

Expressing Disapproval — Page 46

1. Write to their congressmen, circulate petitions, make phone calls to their representatives' offices
2. When the President is given legislation passed by Congress shortly before it adjourns, he may simply do nothing. If he doesn't have ten days while Congress is still in session to voice his objections, then his silence has the effect of a veto. Then the bill does not become a law.
3. It carries quite a bit of clout. The President is his party's leader, and a veto by him brings out a lot of party loyalty when an attempt is made to override his veto.
4. Some of the bills which have no effect on the public are allowed to become law without his signature simply to save time. This silence has the same effect as his signing the bills so long as Congress is in session.
5. To serve as a check against the power of Congress

Express Powers of Congress — Page 50

1. 7
2. 8
3. 6
4. 2
5. 4
6. 1
7. 10
8. 15
9. 11
10. 13
11. 17
12. 9
13. 14
14. 16
15. 12
16. 3
17. 5

"Express vs. Implied" Power — Page 52

1. Express powers are those specifically noted. Implied powers are the additional powers Congress was given by the framers of the Constitution to deal with matters that would emerge. Examples will vary, but our space program would be a good example of an area where Congress has authority that was not specifically pointed out in Section 8.
2. By issuing government bonds to the private sector
3. A person must live in the U.S. for five years, pass a test on the U.S. Constitution plus other requirements.
4. Patents are issued to protect inventions. Copyrights protect books, songs and other written material. The idea is to protect the genius of those who spend their time creating and to prevent others from profiting from their work.

What Congress Cannot Do — Page 56

1. A bill of attainder is a law directed at a specific individual. Ex post facto makes it against the law to have done something in the past that wasn't illegal at the time. This paragraph was included because both were methods used by the British to quiet undesirables in Colonial America.
2. Proof that an individual is being jailed without probable good cause
3. Choosing 1808 as the date when slave trading would become legal was a way of satisfying both slaveholders and those against slavery. In reality it only prolonged the confrontation.

4. Permissions to allow private citizens to capture enemy ships in exchange for the captured cargo, the idea being that supplies for the enemy not received would diminish its chance for success. However, the framers of the Constitution felt that it was like letting people take the law into their own hands and legalizing piracy.
5. The philosophy dates back to the bitterness felt when England ruled over the colonies and granted titles of nobility to those who kept the colonists in line and didn't cause any trouble.
6. The original Constitution stated that all direct taxes must be the same for everyone. The 16th Amendment provides for tax based on a person's wealth, which varies according to income.

Looking back at . . . Article II, Section 1 — Page 61

1. Many of the people in the new nation could not read or write, and they were poorly informed of the affairs of the day because there was little media coverage.

Page 62

2. The President was the man with the most electoral votes. The Vice-President was the runner-up. These two men were expected to work together. There would naturally be resentment by the Vice-President, and the two were more often than not political enemies. The President and Vice-President now run as a team on the same political ticket.
3. The President is a check against the power of Congress. He would always be trying to please them to get a pay raise and avoid a pay cut.
4. Answers will vary.

A Man of Many Hats — Page 64

1. f
2. a/e
3. g
4. b
5. c
6. d
7. e
8. f
9. g
10. b
11. a/c
12. g
13. a
14. f
15. a
16. d
17. g
18. d
19. e/d
20. a

All the President's Men — Page 67

1. f
2. b
3. c
4. i
5. d
6. k
7. e
8. l
9. g
10. h
11. m
12. a
13. j

Looking back on . . . Article II, Sections 2-4 — Page 72

1. What is the main function of the Executive Department?
2. Who is the head of the executive branch of our government?
3. What is the President's title as the chief enforcer of the law?
4. What is the President's title as head of the armed forces?
5. What is the length of the President's term of office?
6. What is the title of the President's assistant?
7. What is the number of electors a state has?
8. When is Inauguration Day?
9. What are the qualifications for becoming President?
10. What do we call the President's group of chief advisors?
11. What vote is required to confirm treaties made by the President with foreign nations?
12. What is defined as betraying one's country?
13. Who actually elects the President?
14. How many members are in the President's cabinet?
15. Who administers the oath of office?
16. What vote is required to confirm appointments made by the President?
17. What is the total number of electors?

Becoming a Federal Judge — Page 78

1. It is an attempt to divorce judges from any political association. Once chosen, the idea is to let them do what they are hired to do—make judicial decisions and not be concerned with the politics associated with being reelected.
2. Some stay on too long and become too old to do a good job. It's also difficult without an election to get rid of someone who doesn't do a good job.
3. impeachment, early retirement
4. a. appointment by the President
   b. confirmation by the Senate

Pinpointing Jurisdiction — Page 80

3. a. appellate
   b. appellate
   c. original
   d. appellate

4. a. U.S. District Court   Page 80
   b. Supreme Court
   c. Circuit Court
   d. U.S. Senate

The System at Work   Page 82
Judicial over Executive d, l
Judicial over Legislative d
Legislative over Judicial a, c, m
Legislative over Executive c, e, h, i, j
Executive over Judicial f, g, o
Executive over Legislative f, b, k, n, o

The Checks of Power   Page 83
1. legislative over executive
2. judicial over legislative, judicial over executive
3. executive over judicial
4. legislative over judicial
5. executive over legislative, judicial over legislative
6. legislative over executive
7. legislative over executive
8. executive over legislative
9. executive over judicial
10. legislative over judicial

Looking back at . . . Original vs. Appellate   Page 84
1. Supreme
2. District
3. Circuit
4. 96
5. 11
6. original
7. appellate
8. judicial review
9. jury
10. 9
11. treason
12. corruption of blood
13. 2
14. life
15. judge
16. simple majority, 5-4
17. unanimous, 12-0
18. appointment by President, approval by the Senate
19. impeachment by the House, conviction by the Senate
20. Chief Justice

Full Faith and Credit Clause   Page 87
1. Each state had its own rules and tariffs to help its own citizens and discriminate against citizens of other states. The Constitution was designed to make each state recognize and value the rules and regulations of all other states.
2. Maine was split from Massachusetts in 1820. West Virginia was divided into West Virginia and Virginia in 1863 following the outbreak of the Civil War.
3. In a true democracy all the people make the rules. The size of the population would not make a true democracy possible in the United States. That's why the people elect their lawmakers.

Amending the Constitution   Page 89
1. 26
2. 26 by Congress, 0 by special conventions
3. 25 by state legislatures, 1 by state conventions
4. 7 years
5. 38
6. There were many issues, but most centered around the controversy of the rights and status of women once they achieved equality. ERA never reached the necessary approval even though it was very close at times. Congress extended the deadline because of this.

General Provisions   Page 91
1. It was our announcement to the world that we would honor all debts accrued prior to the adoption of the Constitution.
2. $80 million
3. Answer will vary according to year, but today's debt is many times greater.
4. The Constitution always rules.
5. They wanted a complete separation of church and state.
6. It points to the Constitution as the Supreme Law of the Land rather than allowing the state to have rights that superseded federal laws.

Ratifying Article VII   Page 93
1. That it would have to be approved by nine of the twelve states who were represented at the Convention
2. 12
3. Rhode Island
4. Pennsylvania
5. 39
6. Delaware, just three minutes after the Convention ended
7. From September 1787 until June 1788. It went into effect in April 1789.

Looking back on . . . Articles IV, V, VI, VII   Page 94
1. extradition
2. 9
3. Article 4
4. Congress
5. Maine and West Virginia
6. Congress
7. 39
8. September 17, 1787
9. 38
10. 26
11. proposal, ratification
12. $80 million
13. Rhode Island
14. 2/3 of Congress, legislatures in 2/3 of the states call for a special convention
15. 3/4 of the state legislatures, conventions in 3/4 of the states
16. Congress
17. U.S. Constitution
18. 1789
19. republic
20. governor of the state

The Bill of Rights   Page 102
1st Amendment
1. a. speech
   b. press
   c. religion
   d. petition
   e. assembly
2. That which is said must either be true or it must not harm anyone.
3. A possible lawsuit in civil court for slander or for libel (written or printed statements, oral statements)
4. If a practice of his religion is against the law
5. To assemble is to gather within a group to discuss issues (soap box style). To petition is to circulate a written statement for the purpose of gaining signatures of those who are either for or against an issue.

2nd Amendment
1. That a person has a right to keep and bear arms to defend himself
2. gun registration laws

3rd Amendment   Page 103
Probably from the people of Boston. No person shall be forced to house military soldiers in his home without permission.

4th Amendment
1. A person's papers, his home, his possessions, his person, his other "personal effects"
2. The date, the expected find, the location, a judge's signature, and the area to be searched

5th Amendment
1. A capital crime is a crime involving the death penalty as punishment. An infamous crime is a serious crime such as murder, robbery, rape, etc., as opposed to a misdemeanor which is a minor crime.
2. A formal accusation charging the accused with a crime and ordering him to be bound over for trial
3. To examine the evidence against the accused to determine if there is enough damaging evidence against him to merit the case going to court
4. 12-23, usually 23
5. A "true bill" means that the grand jury did find enough valid evidence to bring the accused before the court to trial. A "no true bill" means that there is not enough evidence to merit a trial, so the case is dismissed.
   Page 104
6. That no person may be tried for the same crime more than once, assuming that he was found innocent the first time
7. That the defendant is *not* required to give testimony against himself which might lead to his conviction
8. The entire court's procedure, i.e., trial by jury, right to defense, etc.

6th Amendment
1. The trial shall take place in the state where the crime was committed.
2. So secret witnesses cannot bear witness against the accused
3. subpoena

7th Amendment
1. $20
2. a. where there was a question on a point of law
   b. where there has been a technical injustice in the court procedure

8th Amendment
Page 105
1. Money provided by the accused to insure that the defendant will appear before the court at his appointed hour and date
2. Pulling out fingernails, stocks, pillory, lopping off ears and hands, etc.
3. Answers will vary.

9th Amendment
1. Answers will vary.
2. It provides for implied rights, just as Article 1, Section 8 provides for implied power.

10th Amendment
They are reserved for the states and the people.

Our Living Bill of Rights
Page 106
1. 1st Amendment—People have the right to assemble peacefully to protest their government as long as they are not violent and suggest overthrowing the government.
2. 4th Amendment—A warrant must contain exactly what the authorities expect to find.
3. 9th Amendment—One of the unlisted rights which an individual still has is the pursuit of happiness.
Page 107
4. 8th Amendment—The punishment must suit the crime.
5. 3rd Amendment—Quartering of soldiers in private homes is not allowed during peacetime.
6. 6th Amendment—He has the right to subpoena witnesses into court who have something to say on his behalf.
Page 108
7. 5th Amendment—The government does have the right to take the land of a private individual but must pay a fair price for it, which is usually determined by the courts.
8. 2nd Amendment—Julie needs a permit to carry a loaded weapon, even if it is for her own self-defense.
9. 9th Amendment—Both parties have a right to a trial by jury.
10. 10th Amendment

The Birth of Political Parties
Page 113
1. Pros: Conflict of ideas and values should keep both on their toes and provide for an honest government. Cons: Constant quarreling and a lack of harmony. People under such an administration are unsure of what really is the political philosophy of the day.
2. It became clear that there would be many more ties because giving each elector two votes would result in his party loyalty dictating that he vote for both his party's candidates.
3. The two ended up in a pistol duel in which Burr killed Hamilton.

Looking back at . . . Amendments 11 and 12
Page 114
1. That they cannot be heard in federal courts
2. They thought it gave the federal courts too much power.
3. the Electoral College, the Electoral College
4. the state legislatures
5. the people
6. By winning a majority of the electors
7. By winning a majority of the electors
8. The candidate for President who received the second greatest number of electors became Vice-President.
9. There are now candidates who run for Vice-President. Each party ticket contains a candidate for President and one for Vice-President. Whichever party wins the most electors then gets both the President and Vice-President.

Election Day
Page 116
1. The emerging of political parties
2. 538
3. 270
4. Because of the winner-take-all philosophy, it is important to win as many of the big states as possible.
5. Answers will vary according to most recent census and reassignments of electors.
6. Every state has two U.S. senators and at least one representative.

The End of Slavery
Page 121
1. In payment of a debt to society as punishment for committing a crime against that society—prison

2. Being born in the United States and becoming "naturalized" through the satisfaction of certain citizenship requirements among them a test and certain residency requirements
3. To give Blacks a greater status in society—to upgrade them to the level of American citizenship and to reverse the Dred Scott decision
4. No longer can Blacks be counted as 3/5 like property. They shall *all* be counted as full-fledged American citizens.
5. 21 years old, male inhabitant, citizen of the United States, can't have participated in crimes against the United States
6. The the state's representation in the House shall be cut proportionally.
7. 2/3
Page 122
8. The South could *not* pay any of its war debts, and the North's debts would *all* be honored and paid in full.
9. To protect the voting rights of minority groups and to give Blacks an upgraded status
10. To include not only Blacks but other minorities as well
11. The South harbored many feelings of ill will some of which remain today.

Amendment 17
Page 124
1. Prior to the 17th Amendment they were chosen by the state legislature. Now they are elected by the people.
2. The governor can call for a special election, or the governor appoints someone to serve until the next general election when someone will be elected to finish the unexpired term.

Amendment 18
Page 125
The date was 1919. At that time there were 48 states. It required the legislatures of 36 states to approve.

Progressive Era
Page 126
During the early part of the 20th century, many people were working toward important reform movements. Much was needed in the way of reform as there was a lot of corruption in both business and politics. It was also a time when giant strides were being made in science and industries. The Progressives wanted the same kind of progress to take place in government. The common ground that linked the various private interest groups was that they all wanted a better way of life for Americans.

Women Suffrage
Page 128
1. Elizabeth Cady Stanton
2. She fought for better working conditions for women, unions for women, and against alcohol.
3. She died in 1906. The amendment was ratified in 1920.
4. Answers will vary according to the year.
5. The women's vote is very significant.

Lame Duck Amendment
Page 131
1. once each year
2. Prior to the amendment it was November to March 4; now it's from November to January 20 for the President. Prior to the amendment it was November until the next December; now it's from November to January 3 for Congress.
3. Congress will decide.
4. It's an ineffective time when the old Congress and President are pretty much without power.

Repeal of Prohibition—Amendment 21
Page 133
1. Americans had no desire to be told what to do. World War I had just ended and people felt it was time to have fun. Also there weren't enough federal agents to enforce the mechanics of the Volstead Act.
2. Members of Congress felt that it was public pressure that had brought about the 18th Amendment in the first place. It was now public pressure that was bringing an end to Prohibtion. The feeling was that the people themselves ought to have a hand in the final decision. So they chose the convention method where private individuals would be chosen as delegates.
3. It is against Communism, monopoly, gambling, pornography, drugs and socialized medicine.

Looking back at . . . the 22nd Amendment
Page 135
1. Franklin D. Roosevelt was elected President four times. Many people felt that was too long for one person to serve as President of the United States.
2. Dwight D. Eisenhower
3. He could serve up to two years of another elected President's term; then he could be elected to the office twice himself.
4. Yes, he could run in 1976 and did, but he lost to Jimmy Carter. If he had been elected in 1976, he could not have run in 1980 because the combined time would have given him longer than ten years as President.
5. Answers will vary, but discussion should involve both the advantages as well as the disadvantages of having the same leader for a long period of time.

Amendment 23
Page 136
1. It has the same number as the smallest state. The least number a state can have is three (i.e., every state has two senators and at least one representative).
2. 538
3. 270

Amendment 24
Page 137
1. Mainly to discriminate against poor Blacks who could not pay the tax.
2. In most state elections, national officials would be elected at the same time, and the state would have to print two separate ballots.

Presidential Disability
Page 140
1. In 1973 Vice-President Spiro Agnew resigned. President Nixon appointed Gerald Ford as Vice-President. In August of 1974, Nixon resigned as President and Gerald Ford became President. Ford then chose Nelson Rockefeller to serve as his Vice-President.
2. He must have agreement from a majority of the cabinet. Then to keep him out as President, the matter goes before a vote of Congress.
3. He merely notifies the leaders of both houses of Congress.
4. His doctor would be the best judge.

Amendment 26
Page 141
1. The law said that 18-year-olds could not be barred from voting for national officials. If states which had different age requirements were to keep their own minimum age standards for voting for state and local officials, they would need separate ballots and voting lists for those below their age requirements and those who had qualified.

Our Amendments at Work
Page 142
1. 4
2. 9
3. 15
4. 17
5. 19
6. 6
7. 1
8. 7

Page 143
9. 12
10. 14
11. 24
12. 20
13. 5
14. 2
15. 3
16. 16
17. 26

Page 144
18. 23
19. 11
20. 22
21. 18
22. 21
23. 25
24. 8
25. 13
26. 10

Looking back on . . . the Constitution
Page 145
1. Article 1, Section 8, clause 3. Congress can control trade.
2. Article 1, Section 2, clause 1. House members are chosen every two years.
3. Article 1, Section 7, clause 3. Congress needs approval by the President on all matters except impeachment.
4. 6th Amendment. The accused has the right to be confronted with witnesses against him.
5. Article 3, Section 1. Federal judges serve for life.
6. Article 2, Section 2, clause 2. Simple majority of the Senate.
Page 146
7. 25th Amendment, Section 4. If a majority of the cabinet agrees that the President is unable to return, it notifies Congress. It takes 2/3 of each house to keep him out.
8. Article 2, Section 1, clause 5. The minimum age for a President is 35 years old.
9. Article 2, Section 1, clause 2. In such case, the President is elected by the House of Representatives.
10. Article 4, Section 2, clause 2. A fleeing criminal can be apprehended and returned to the state where he is accused on demand of the governor.
11. Article 2, Section 2, clause 1. The President shall be Commander in Chief of the armed forces.
12. 2nd Amendment. The right of the people to keep and bear arms shall not be infringed.
13. Article 1, Section 2, clause 4. The House of Representatives shall have the sole power of impeachment.
Page 147
14. 22nd Amendment. No President may be elected more than twice nor serve more than ten years.
15. 8th Amendment. Excessive bail and fines are not allowed.
16. Article 3, Section 3, clause 1. No person shall be convicted of treason without the testimony of two eyewitnesses or an open confession.
17. Article 4, Section 3, clause 1. New states may be admitted into the Union by Congress.
18. Article 5. Three-fourths of the state legislatures are required to ratify amendments.
19. 5th Amendment. The right of eminent domain gives the government the right to take land of private individuals for the good of all, but a just price must be paid.
20. Article 1, Section 10, clause 1. No state may coin money.

LESSON PLANNER

Assignment	Date(s) Assigned	Teacher Notes/Comments
Introduction		
Prelude to Independence		
Declaration of Independence		
The Road to Change		
Drawing Conclusions		
Preamble		
Article I—Legislative Department		
Article II—Executive Department		
Article III—Judicial Department		
Article IV—The Relation of the States		
Article V—Amending the Constitution		
Article VI—General Provisions		
Article VII—Ratification		
Bill of Rights		
Amendments 11 and 12		
Slavery Amendments—13, 14, 15		
Progressive Amendments—16, 17, 18, 19		
Amendment 20		
Amendment 21		
Amendment 22		
Amendment 23		
Amendment 24		
Amendment 25		
Amendment 26		
We the People		